What's Cookin' in ARIZONA!

More than 240 recipes from

Arizona Celebrities & Personalities

Compiled

by

Sandy Bruce

GOLDEN WEST ✶ PUBLISHERS

Cover art and interior caricatures by Mike Ritter

Note: All signatures in this book have been electronically reproduced.

Bruce, Sandy
What's Cookin' in Arizona! : Favorite recipes from Arizona Celebrities
& Personalities / by Sandy Bruce.
     p.   cm.
Includes index.
ISBN 0-914846-88-4
1. Cookery—Arizona.   2. Celebrities—Arizona.   I. Title.
TX715.2.A6B78   1993   93-37691
641.59791—dc20   CIP

Printed in the United States of America

ISBN # 0-914846-88-4

Information in this book is deemed to be authentic and accurate by
author and publisher. However, they disclaim any liability incurred
in connection with the use of information appearing in this book.

Golden West Publishers, Inc.
4113 N. Longview Ave.
Phoenix, AZ 85014, USA

(602) 265-4392

IN THE BEGINNING...

You would think that collecting recipes from Arizona folks would be a simple and relatively uncomplicated task. At least I did. Little did I know! Not only are Arizonans a diverse and fascinating collection of individuals—and individualists—they also can be hard to get hold of, and, sometimes, hard to distract from their pursuits in order to capture their attention....as in, distracting them long enough to get them to send me recipes for this book.

Tracking down celebrities who hail from Arizona was one of the more challenging tasks in assembling the recipes for this book. I knew, for instance, that Linda Ronstadt was a native of Tucson, so I wanted her recipe. But how to get in touch with her? I did it the old fashioned way: I called every single Ronstadt in Tucson until I finally located a distant relative who gave me the name of her manager in California, who rounded up Linda's fabulous recipe for corn muffins. After many tries with Steven Spielberg's assistant, I decided to give up, only because he was in Poland starting a new film. I tried for months to contact Alice Cooper, who lives here and is seen frequently on Valley golf courses, but I struck out with his very protective agent. An item in a newspaper column about the preparations for this book led to a phone call from a gentleman who said he played golf with Alice weekly. He said he'd be happy to help out. But, as of press time, no tamale. Maybe for the next edition. I know, Alice: I am not worthy . . . but I'd still like to know your favorite dish—something from the 19th hole, perhaps?

On the other hand, some famous names with Arizona connections were remarkably easy. I wrote to Erma Bombeck's newspaper syndicate with a request for a recipe, and she responded immediately. Barry Goldwater, likewise, was quick with his formula for *Arizona Chili*. I asked my husband to hand Walter Cronkite a request when he was in Phoenix on behalf of the ASU journalism school, which is named in his honor. While it took a few months and more than a few phone calls, Walter's recipe for *Herring Copenhagen* finally arrived in the mail. (Walter told my husband, Jeff, that a recipe for *Harvard Beets* is sometimes connected to his name. Just for the record, "the most trusted man in America" isn't really all that fond of Harvard Beets, whatever they are.)

I knew this cookbook wouldn't be complete without representation from the Phoenix Suns. I sent letters through the Suns' corporate offices to all the players, but, like so much unanswered fan mail, most of mine was more than likely in a pile somewhere. I soon realized I'd have to pick my targets. My first chance came at, of all places, an Arizona State University basketball game when Dan Majerle showed up unexpectedly at the scorer's table. He was quickly beset by autograph seekers, and I had a fan (my husband) hand him my business card with a cryptic note on the back asking for his recipe. A few weeks later, his mother was in town visiting Dan and she gave me a call His recipe for *Strawberry Cream Squares* arrived shortly thereafter. I even tried handing personal letters to a Suns player who was scheduled for a personal appearance at a Scottsdale mall — but never heard back from him or the sought-after Gorilla. Eventually, the wives of Paul Westphal, Mark West and Cotton Fitzsimmons called me to add to the Suns recipe roster.

Former Vice President Dan Quayle spent much of his youth in Arizona and his family owns one of the state's larger newspapers. A recipe from him was a must. Shortly after the November 1992 election, I sent a letter to his Washington, D.C. office, but drew a blank. Then, I obtained the fax number for his wife, Marilyn's, law firm in Indianapolis, and became a pest on the fax machine. It paid off when the Quayle's favorite recipe for orange rolls rolled in.

Of course, not everyone who submitted recipes for this book is a household name. Do the names Ted Conibear, or Ivan Reece or Tanner Burgard sound familiar? Well, if you've ever driven through Oak Creek Canyon you've no doubt seen Mr. Conibear's magnificent sand sculptures alongside the road. Ivan Reece's claim to fame is as an egg carton sculptor and Tanner Burgard is the world's youngest water skier. Then again, not all the recipes contained herein are from people: check out the recipe from Ruby the Elephant for *Bananas Glazed With Guava Rum*; or Alex the Gibbon Ape's recipe for *Fruit, Fruit and More Fruit!*

All told, it took nine months to track down all the recipes for this book. In so doing, I learned a lot. It's easier to reach the Vice President than an Indian chief. Some of the most famous people in

Arizona are also the most friendly. Some of the people who need public recognition the most — a goodly number of politicians come to mind —are, ironically, the least likely to take advantage of a little free publicity. Fencing with overprotective secretaries is an unspeakable aggravation. A surprising number of well known folks answer their own phones and their own mail. There are several big-name sports celebrities in this state, who, despite their public persona, you wouldn't invite into your home if you knew them. There are many, many more common folk that all of us would be blessed to know better.

This book is modeled after "The Congressional Club Cookbook," a wonderful collection of recipes from members of Congress and their families. I ran across the congressional cookbook during a trip to the nation's capitol, and was inspired by the idea of creating a similar work for Arizona. I wanted to do something to celebrate the wonderful people of our state. I hope you'll see this as more than a collection of things to eat, but, rather, a cookbook AND a collection of tidbits about the fascinating people who inhabit our beautiful corner of the Southwest. Some of the biographical entries go into great detail, others are quite brief. My intent was not to "grade" the significance of the generous people who took the time to donate their recipes to this book, but, rather, to offer some glimpses into the diverse makeup of our state.

It should be noted that all the royalties from the first 10,000 copies of this book will be donated directly to Women Off Welfare, a charitable organization based in Mesa that is dedicated to helping men and women who have fallen on hard times get their lives back together. Unquestionably, the fact that these proceeds are to be donated to this worthy cause motivated many of the responses for recipes for this book, and for that generosity on the part of the contributors to "What's Cookin' in Arizona" I am deeply grateful.

Sandy Bruce

WOW!

Fear, anger and abuse are typical problems of today's family environment for many people. Mary Ruiz, now a single mother, is well aware of the devastating effects of physical and emotional abuse and family difficulties. Mary, a mother of four children, was left destitute with no transportation, unpaid bills, the inability to work, family crisis and a lack of self-esteem.

Women Off Welfare (WOW!) deals with families in this situation on a daily basis: victims of abuse and devastating circumstances. The result, most often, is welfare — an average income of less than $400 a month on which to survive and keep a family together. Welfare dependency and desperation creates feelings of being trapped with no way out.

There is a way out, however. WOW!, a demonstration project sponsored by the Mesa United Way, together with an alliance of community resources, has helped hundreds of single mothers like Mary to get off welfare and get their lives back on track. The mission of WOW! is to rebuild their lives through job training, education, self-esteem building, job placement and support services to get off welfare and get back into the community as contributing members of society.

Through the services provided by the WOW! program, Mary now has a job and is getting back on her feet both financially and emotionally. She says: "With the helping hand of WOW!, I now have my self-esteem and an assurance that I can do it."

The purchase of this cookbook will assist WOW! in helping many more women like Mary find success, self-esteem, dignity and, most importantly, self-sufficiency. WOW!

Table of Contents

(See Index to Recipe Contributors - - page 14)

Breakfasts

Appetizers

Soups & Chili

Salads & Dressings

Sauces & Relishes

Breads

Main Dishes

Side Dishes

Desserts

Beverages

Index to Recipe Contributors

Recipe Contributors continued . . .

Olson, R. Luther "Lute" 70
Onodera, Rosalind Ong   136
Opsahl, H. M. (Butch)   65
Osman, Herbert E.   51
Owens, Steve   228
Palmer, Leah Wheatley   159
Parks Jr., Ray S.   203
Payne, Coy   220
Peralta, E. J. "Dolli"   168
Pickens, Marion L.   229
Pomeroy, Ralph   139
Pooley, Don   36
Pranspill, George O.   81
Purtzer, Tom   238
Quayle, Dan   91
Reece, Ivan W.   69
Reid, Larry   96
Rhodes III, John J.   23
Risseeuw, John   154
Ritter, Mike   243
Roberts, Junith H.   95
Romley, Richard M.   153
Ronstadt, Linda   94
Rubach, Peggy   183
Ruland-Thorne, Kate   144
Rutkowski, Daiton   19
Salmon, Matt   227
Sandler, Ronald   158
Schnepf, Mark   151
Schultz, Buddy   149
Scott, Jerry   162
Seymann, Marilyn R.   93
Shepherd, Lin Sue   40
Shields, Robert   199
Shiery, Carol A.   219
Shocket, Kathy   163
Siegel, Jeffrey   152
Smith, Diana   68
Smith, Edward A.   150
Smith, Harvey K.   92
Smith, Tom   155
Solomon, Ruth   200

Sossaman, James J.   201
Springer, Carol   42
Stapley, James P. "Jim"   226
Steffey, Lela   202
Stephens, Alan   42
Stevenson, Linda Jo   38
Stewart, Sr., Warren H.   235
Stump, Bob   148
Swanson, Ray   191
Symington, Ann & Fife   147
Taylor, Dan & Martha   146
Taylor, Janet   22
Thomson, June   160
Thor, Linda M.   193
Threadgill, James   97
Tippett, Robert H.   145
Todd, Christi   225
Tolby, Quentin V.   200
Torrey, Bill   197
Trimble, Marshall   192
Turk, Rudy   233
Van Camp, Cathy   204
Van Dyke, Vonda   50
Vaughan, Keith   143
Vaughan, Robert A.   21
Vonier, Richard S. &
    Donald Downes   164
Waddell, John   100
Walters, Tony   241
Weil III, Louis A.   242
Wennes, Howie E.   189
Wessel, Nancy   67
West, Mark   206
Westmoreland, Preston   161
Westphal, Paul   41
Whalen, Martin J.   53
White, Danny   73
Willey, Keven   142
Wong, Willie   141
Woods, Grant   224
Wright, Patricia "Pat"   189
Yarnell, Lorene   172

RECIPE FOR A HAPPY DAY

- **1 kiss for each spouse and each child**
- **3 hugs for any child who looks like he/she needs it**
- **say "Hello" to everyone**
- **try to listen instead of talking—70% of the time**
- **call your spouse twice a day to say "I love you"**
- **cuddle a pet twice a day**
- **open a door for everyone**
- **hold an infant and talk babytalk to it**
- **cry—about anything sad**
- **laugh so hard that you cry**
- **tell one joke a day**
- **learn a new word**
- **call your mom/dad to tell them you love them**

G. Robert Meko

G. Robert Meko

Bob Meko is the principal of Ramon S. Mendoza Elementary School in Mesa. And a bald one at that, for a while. Meko shared this story: *"Charles Barkley agreed to shave my head if Mendoza set a new state record for collecting canned food—15,000 cans. Mr. Barkley wanted to visit my school quietly—with no T.V., cameras or flashing lights. He pulled up to my school in a green Mercedes with the humble attitude of a hard-working man. He showed respect to all he met. As he took the razor down the center of my scalp he seemed shocked and said 'Wow'. Mr. Charles Barkley left for the Mendoza Community a memory which will last forever. A memory of helping so many others through our hard work and of a quiet man who quietly praised us for doing so."*

THE BEST PANCAKES IN THE WEST

1 egg
1 C. milk
1 C. plain yogurt
4 Tbsp. molasses
1 C. rye flour (stone ground is best)
1 C. white flour
1 tsp. baking powder
1/2 tsp. salt
1 tsp. soda

Add beaten egg to milk, yogurt and molasses. Beat again to mix. In another bowl, combine all the dry ingredients. Add the dry mixture to the liquids gradually and stir to mix well. It may be necessary to add more milk. Fry on a hot greased griddle or skillet. This pancake mix works best when it is a little thinner than some pancake mixes and when you make small, thin pancakes about 3" to 4" diameter. Great with real maple syrup or fresh raspberry jam!

Jane Metzger

Jane Metzger

Jane Metzger is an artist who has been involved in the Arizona art community since 1969. She has been especially interested in developing the awareness of fine crafts in Arizona and has been active in Arizona Designer Craftsmen for many years. In addition to numerous exhibitions of her multi-media art, she will also be serving on the Visual Arts Panel of the Arizona Commission on the Arts.

OATMEAL

1 C. oatmeal • 1 1/4 C. water • 1/2 tsp. salt

Cook slowly for 15 minutes.

Ted Conibear

Ted Conibear

Ted Conibear is the Sedona sand sculptor whose works are on display just at the base of Oak Creek Canyon. The sand sculptures depict the Last Supper and Jesus Christ. If you have ever traveled through Sedona you have probably seen his work. The sand he uses for his sculptures is from the cliffs and creeks nearby. His tools are a paring knife, teaspoon, and two brushes. This work will last indefinitely if protected from wind and rain. (Author's note: My family was driving through the area last summer and stopped at the sculptures to take a few pictures. Mr. Conibear, a native of Canada, was there checking on his statues. He told me he had just turned 86 years old on July 31.)

DEAD EYE DICK

butter • slice of bread • 1 egg

Using a small skillet, melt a generous amount of butter over relatively high heat. Take a slice of bread, tear out a hole in the center (size of 1/2 dollar), dip both sides of bread in the butter, lay in pan and break the egg into the center of the bread. Fry until crisp on both sides. Serve with favorite condiment.

Daiton Rutkowski

Daiton Rutkowski is the mayor of the city of Prescott.

ARIZONA SOUFFLÉ

1 sm. can chopped green chiles
sliced Jack cheese
tomatoes, sliced thin
1 1/2 dozen eggs
salt and Accent® to taste

Spread chile in bottom of a buttered baking dish (9 x 13). Lay slices of Jack cheese on top of chile. Layer tomatoes on top of cheese. Beat eggs until frothy, adding salt and Accent to taste. Pour over other ingredients. Bake at 350 degrees for 30 to 40 minutes or until set.

Joe D. Lloyd

Joe D. Lloyd

Joe Lloyd is the chairman of the Department of Performing Arts and Director of Bands at Red Mountain High School. He is also director of the Northern Arizona University Summer Music Camp and treasurer of the Arizona Music Educators Association. He was Arizona Music Educator of the year (1991) and received the National Federation of State High School Associations Outstanding Music Educator Award.

GOOD MORNING SHORTCAKE

1 C. flour
1 Tbsp. baking powder
1/2 tsp. salt
1 C. quick-cooking oats
3 Tbsp. oil
1 beaten egg
1/3 C. milk
2 Tbsp. honey

Stir dry ingredients together.

Combine oil, egg, milk, and honey; add all at once to dry mixture. Stir just till moist. Drop by spoonfuls on greased baking sheet. Bake in 425 degree oven for 12 to 15 minutes for 6 cakes, 8 to 10 minutes for smaller ones.

Split shortcakes, then fill and top with fruit such as peaches, berries, bananas or pears, and add whipped topping or ice cream.

You may use whole wheat flour with this recipe or use 3/4 cup white flour and 1/4 cup wheat germ.

This is a favorite special breakfast for children and adults in our family.

Robert A. Vaughan

Robert Vaughan is the executive director of the Yuma Metropolitan Planning Organization.

CHRIS'S
SUNDAY BREAKFAST PANCAKE

Preheat oven to 425 degrees.

1/2 C. flour	few grates fresh nutmeg
1/2 C. milk	2 Tbsp. butter
2 eggs	juice from 1/2 lemon
dash salt	powdered sugar

In medium size bowl mix flour, milk, eggs, salt and nutmeg. Mix lightly with whisk. Spray skillet with vegetable spray, then melt butter over heat. Add mixture and pop into oven.

After about 15 to 20 minutes, this pancake will rise into a golden shape. Cut fresh lemon in half and squeeze juice and strain. Remove pancake from oven and sprinkle juice over pancake. The pancake will deflate so sprinkle powdered sugar over it and return to oven for about 5 minutes.

Remove from oven and place on platter. Cut into wedges and serve with more powdered sugar or homemade jam. Accompany this with bacon or sausage and fresh fruit and juice.

Janet Taylor

Janet Taylor

Janet Taylor is a professor of art at Arizona State University School of Art. She recently opened her own weaving studio in Tempe where she works with students who help with the commissioned tapestries and fabrics that are produced for custom designed interiors. Janet's work is displayed in many buildings throughout the Valley, as well as in other parts of the United States.

SOUFFLÉ de la SOUTHWEST

1 can (4 oz.) green chiles, chopped
1 lb. Jack cheese, thinly sliced
4 tomatoes, thinly sliced
18 eggs
salt and pepper to taste

Spread chiles in bottom of greased 9 x 13 baking dish. Cover with layer of cheese slices. Top with layer of tomato slices. Beat eggs until frothy. Add salt and pepper to taste. Pour over other ingredients. Bake in 350 degree oven for 35 minutes or until eggs are set.

John J. Rhodes III

Jay Rhodes of Mesa is an attorney and former United States congressman. He is currently of counsel in Washington, D.C.

BREAKFAST BURRITOS

(A true southwestern breakfast!)

4 to 6 eggs
1 Tbsp. butter
vegetables, sliced or diced*

cheese, shredded
salsa, hot or mild
4 to 6 flour tortillas

Melt butter in heated skillet. Sauté onions until translucent. Add peppers, mushrooms and favorite vegetables. While vegetables are still crisp add beaten eggs and scramble to desired consistency. Remove from heat. Warm tortillas (stovetop, oven or microwave). Place heated tortilla flat on plate, add egg mixture, top with grated cheese, add salsa or other condiments and roll up burrito-style.

For serving, top with any of the following: salsa, sour cream, sprouts, sliced avocado, cheese sauce.

*Filling suggestions: onions, bell peppers (red or green), mushrooms, diced chiles, diced potatoes, zucchini, eggplant.

Note: this is a great way to utilize leftovers! Just about anything in the refrigerator can be added to these burritos. Especially tasty are leftover cooked meats including steak, prime rib (cut into very small pieces), ham, chicken, turkey, lobster and crab.

If the burritos are rolled securely you can eat these by hand. The sensation of holding the warm burrito and savoring its steamy taste is an especially satisfying breakfast experience!

Lee Fischer

Lee Fischer

Lee Fischer is an Arizona native. With his brother, Bruce, he owns Golden West Publishers, a firm specializing in books about Arizona and the southwest. Lee and his wife, Shayne, collaborated on this recipe, but when it comes to who rules in the kitchen the answer is obvious. *"Whenever I'm cooking something I always have to ask where everything is. Shayne can take a plain idea and create an innovative and wonderful dish. I just do the eating!"*

HOT DIGGITY DOG!

Take your favorite beef frank and cut into bite size pieces. Serve with American cheese also cut into bite sizes. Eat as finger foods!

Tanner Burgard

Tanner Burgard of Arizona, is the world's youngest water skier at age 5 months, 19 days. He loves hot dogs! His father says, "*World class water skiers from around the globe have been training on this famous Tanner training diet! Tanner understands the importance of a proper diet while training.*"

POCKET PITA PIZZA

1 whole pocket pita (not pre-sliced)
jar of pizza sauce
shredded mozzarella cheese
option: sliced black olives, green pepper, onions, zucchini

Preheat oven to 425 degrees. Carefully cut the top off the pita bread (do not cut through to bottom). Make a big circle and set the

top aside. Take the pizza sauce and spread it over the bottom of the opened pita. Cover it with the mozzarella cheese. Add any of the optional ingredients. Bake on a cookie sheet in a 425 degree oven for 10 to 15 minutes. Toast the top piece of the pita then place it over the top of the pizza. Enjoy!

Danny Handke

Danny Handke

Danny Handke has been drawing cartoons since he could hold a pencil! He is now ten years old and has already sold a cartoon logo to a local business. He also has redesigned his school mascot and drawn all the cartoons for the school year book. Danny started his own company called FANTAST-A-TOONS™ and has developed many characters, including one pesky little puppy, called Chuck, that somehow resembles his little brother. He plans to continue doing cartoon and logo work and is also teaching cartooning to other children.

ARPAIO'S PETITE MEATBALLS

MEATBALLS
1 lb. ground beef
1/2 C. soft bread crumbs
1/3 C. milk
1/2 tsp. garlic salt
1/2 tsp. onion salt
few drops Tabasco® Sauce
2 Tbsp. olive oil
MUSTARD SAUCE
2 Tbsp. butter
2 Tbsp. regular all purpose flour
1 C. milk
1 Tbsp. prepared mustard

To prepare meatballs: In a bowl lightly mix together beef, crumbs, milk, onion, garlic salt and Tabasco sauce. Form into 40 marble size meatballs. In a skillet, brown meatballs in the olive oil. Keep warm in oven. Serve with wooden pick in each, to be dipped in Mustard Sauce.

To prepare sauce: In a small sauce pan melt butter, blend in flour. Remove from heat. Gradually stir in milk. Cool over medium heat, stirring constantly until thickened. Cook two additional minutes. Stir in mustard. Serve warm.

Joe Arpaio

Joe Arpaio is the sheriff of Maricopa County.

CREAMY CHICKEN NACHOS

1 C. shredded, cooked chicken breast
8 oz. cream cheese, softened
1 jalapeño pepper, seeded and finely chopped
3 Tbsp. finely chopped red onion
2 cloves garlic, finely chopped
1 tsp. cumin seed, crushed to a coarse powder
1 tsp. chili powder
1 1/2 C. Jack cheese
salt and freshly ground pepper to taste
approximately 8 dozen tortilla chips

With an electric mixer, cream together all the ingredients except the tortilla chips until well blended. Refrigerate until ready to use, but bring to room temperature before assembling so that the mixture is spreadable. Preheat broiler. Evenly spread each chip with a generous amount of the mixture. Arrange chips on baking sheet and broil about 3 inches away from the heat until puffed and golden.

Hattie and Bruce Babbitt

Hattie Babbitt is the United States ambassador to the Organization of American States. The Organization of American States is an association designed to promote peace and stability between the United States and Latin American and Caribbean nations. The former Phoenix lawyer speaks Spanish and has extensive experience in Latin American affairs.

Former Arizona Governor Bruce Babbitt is the secretary of the Department of Interior. The Department of the Interior was established in 1849. It is the fifth-ranking executive department. Primary responsibilities include public lands administration, Indian affairs, dam and mine safety, national parks operation, overseas territories supervision and mineral resources management.

This is an appetizer they particularly enjoyed on the evening before they departed for Washington after their appointments by President Bill Clinton.

PHIL AUSTIN'S PHABULOUS & PHESTIVE GUACAMOLE

Historical Anecdote by Phil Austin: Legend has it that guacamole was the Western Hemisphere's equivalent to ambrosia. The chef's detailed historical research revealed no basis in fact for this legend. Historical documents uncovered during a recent archeological excavation revealed that ambrosia was a result of the Ancient Greek's attempt to duplicate the recipe for guacamole created by the indigenous peoples of the Western Hemisphere.

6 ripe avocados
1/2 to 3/4 C. sour cream
juice from 1/2 lemon
pinch of cilantro
pinch of oregano
1 minced clove of garlic
salt for taste
red chile powder or Tabasco® (to suit taste)

Place all the ingredients in a bowl. Best result is to mix with wooden spoon. If you're in a hurry, can blend in blender, but not recommended for optimal results. Serve with corn chips.

Phillip L. Austin

Phil Austin

Phil is the director of community affairs in the Office of the Attorney General. He is past president of the Mesa Association of Hispanic Citizens, and a member of the board of directors of the Mesa Education Foundation.

MARGIE FROST'S CHILI CHEESE BEAN DIP WITH SOUL

2 lbs. ground beef or turkey
1 lb. cheddar cheese grated
1 can diced green chiles
1 onion, chopped
2 - 16 oz. cans refried beans
salt and pepper to taste
1 can stewed tomatoes (broken up with juice)

Brown the meat, drain any grease. Add all other ingredients to meat mixture and simmer gently until cheese is melted.

Serve with corn chips (tortilla that is) or use as a burrito filling. This makes an inexpensive dish to feed a large number of people.

Margie Frost

Margie Frost

Margie Frost is Mesa's 1990 Woman of the Year and is the president of Arizona Community Action Association and the director of Client Services for the Mesa Community Action Agency.

MY ARIZONA PATÉ

2 - 15 oz. cans black beans
1 C. tomatoes, peeled (canned tomatoes)
1 - 10 oz. can RO-TEL® or two cups canned tomatoes and
      8 oz. can green chiles
1 tsp. cumin
1 tsp. chili powder
1 tsp. garlic powder
1 tsp. onion powder

Drain beans. Put all ingredients in a blender and puree. If blender is not available, use a mixer and mix until smooth. Pour into serving dish. Can be used as a dip or on crackers. Ingredients will thicken in the refrigerator. Stir to thin. May add salt to taste. I often add about a teaspoon Tabasco® sauce, but the Paté as it stands does have a "nudge" to it.

Ed Gaia

Ed Gaia is one of the 1992 "12 Who Care Hon Kachina Honorees". According to legend, the Hon Kachina represents great healing powers and symbolizes excellence in volunteer service for the assisting in the healing of others. The Luke's Men of St. Luke's Medical and Behavioral Health Centers and KPNX-Channel 12 annually honor twelve outstanding volunteers for their contributions to humanity. Gaia writes: *"We are running a thrift store in Kingman to get our funds. We are supporting an alcoholic rehab unit which is working out quite well. We hope it soon will be free-standing, because the people who live there really want to straighten their lives out. About 125 individuals have left sober since April 1990. We support a homeless shelter which is doing a good job, too. I would really like to start a Women Off Welfare program up here. We also help transients with gas and food, families with utilities, etc. We don't turn away anyone."*

Ed Gaia

SWEET & SOUR BIRDIE WINGS

36 chicken wings
3 eggs
1 Tbsp. garlic powder

1 1/2 C. cornstarch
oil

SAUCE
3/4 C. chicken broth
3/4 C. catsup
2 1/2 C. sugar
1 1/2 C. vinegar

1 Tbsp. soy sauce
1 Tbsp. salt
1 1/2 tsp. Accent®

Cut tips from wings, then dip wings in lightly beaten eggs. Roll in cornstarch to which garlic has been added. Brown wings in oil. Place in 10 x 10 inch baking dish. Mix all ingredients for sauce and pour over wings. Bake 40 minutes at 375 degrees.

Rose Mofford

Rose Mofford is a former Arizona state governor.

STUFFED MUSHROOMS

1 lb. large mushrooms
1/2 lb. pork sausage
2 Tbsp. finely chopped onion
1 C. soft bread crumbs
1/4 C. chopped parsley
1/2 tsp. seasoned pepper

Clean mushrooms with damp paper towel. (Do not rinse with water.) Sauté sausage (do not brown); drain fat. Remove stems from mushrooms and chop stems fine; add stems and onion to sausage and cook a few minutes. Add 2 tablespoons water and remaining ingredients; use your fingers to thoroughly combine ingredients. Stuff mushrooms and bake in pan with a little water at 375 degrees for 15 minutes.

Dan McCarthy

Dan McCarthy is the editor of the Tempe Daily News Tribune.

CHEESE BALL

4 oz. blue cheese
12 oz. cream cheese
2 sm. jars sharp cheddar cheese spread
1/2 tsp. parsley flakes
1 C. chopped pecans (1/2 C. mixed in cheese mixture
and 1/2 C. reserved for garnish)
1 Tbsp. Worcestershire sauce
1/4 C. onion, finely chopped

Let first three ingredients set out to become room temperature. Combine parsley flakes and pecans, set aside. Mix all ingredients except half of parsley flakes/pecans with electric mixer until well blended. Shape into ball and roll in remaining parsley flakes/pecans.

Guy Meeks

Guy Meeks is the chief of police of the city of Mesa. His professional and civic affiliations include being a member of the International Association of Chiefs of Police; the board of directors of the Arizona Association of Chiefs of Police; and the executive board for "Do Drugs. Do Time". He's also a member of the F.B.I. National Academy Graduate Association; Governor's Drug and Gang Enforcement Task Force; the board of management for Mesa YMCA (chairs a special committee dealing with Youth At Risk) and a member of Mesa Rotary.

COTTAGE CHEESE DIP

1 carton (32 oz.) low fat
  cottage cheese
1 lg. or 2 sm. tomatoes
1 lg. can green chiles

4 to 5 green onions
garlic salt
pepper
tortilla chips

Chop tomatoes, chiles and onions and combine with cottage cheese in a large bowl. Sprinkle garlic salt and pepper over mixture. Mix again. Serve with tortilla chips.

Don Pooley

Don Pooley is one of Arizona's PGA members who turned professional in 1973, the same year he graduated from the University of Arizona in Business Administration. He scored a Million Dollar Hole-in-One at the 1987 Bay Hill Classic where half of the proceeds went to Arnold Palmer's Children's Hospital. Don's tour victories include the 1980 B. C. Open and the 1987 Memorial Tournament. Don lives in Tucson with his wife, Margaret and their two children.

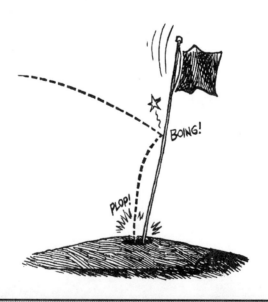

CHICKEN DRUMETTES

3 to 4 dozen drumettes or wings

SAUCE

1 C. brown sugar

1 C. soy sauce

3/4 C. cooking sherry

1/2 tsp. dry mustard

2 cloves garlic, mashed

Mix in saucepan and bring to boil, then pour over chicken and bake in 325 degree oven for 1 1/2 hour.

Christopher J. Bavasi

Christopher Bavasi is the mayor of the city of Flagstaff.

TORTILLA TANTALIZERS

3 pkg. (8 oz.) cream cheese

1 pt. sour cream

1 Tbsp. picante sauce

10 green onions, chopped

4 jalapeños, chopped, no seeds

juice of 1 lime

10 to 12 flour tortillas

Combine all ingredients, except tortillas. Spread mixture on tortillas. Roll (jelly roll fashion). Wrap individually in plastic wrap. Refrigerate several hours, remove plastic wrap, then slice, about 8 to 9 pieces per tortilla.

Sandy Bruce

Sandy Bruce is the author of *What's Cookin' in Arizona!* See "About the Author" on page 251.

LOBSTER CON QUESO

Among the rugged crags of the red canyon walls of Sedona once stood Oak Creek Lodge, famous for two generations of cooks. The Mayhew family opened the lodge when the road was a wagon trail. A Mayhew daughter, Mrs. Al Wohlschlegel, cooking on the original giant wood stove, added lobster to traditional chile con queso. The luxury of lobster, the zip of salsa, and the creamy binding of longhorn cheese make this dish memorable.

1/4 C. chopped green onions with tops
1/2 bell pepper, finely diced
2 Tbsp. corn or olive oil
1 C. green chile salsa
3 C. canned tomatoes, with juice
1 tsp. chili powder
1 C. lobster, cooked and chunked
1 C. grated longhorn cheese
1/2 C. heavy cream
1 loaf fresh crusty bread

Sauté onion and bell pepper in hot oil. When onions are transparent, add salsa and simmer. Dice or chop tomatoes to add to sauce. Cook until tender, adding chili powder. Taste. Add salt and pepper, if necessary. Gently stir in lobster. (Use 1 cup canned lobster if fresh is not available.)

Add grated cheese and the cream. Heat until very hot, stirring with wooden spoon. Transfer to chafing dish and have ready small plates and large chunks of fresh, crusty bread. Guests dip and serve themselves, fondue style. Enough for 8 as an appetizer.

Linda Jo Stevenson

Linda Jo Stevenson co-owns Soderberg/Stevenson Sculpture Galleries in Sedona. Linda Jo is a prime mover in Sedona's gallery association and launched a special art show on KAZM radio that she now hosts.

BACK EAST "CRABBIES"

1/2 lb. crab meat
2 Tbsp. mayonnaise
2 jars Old English® Cheddar Cheese
8 English muffins, split
8 oz. butter, melted
garlic powder (to taste)

Mix crab meat and mayonnaise together. Spread cheese on English muffins and top with crab meat mixture. Drizzle butter over top of crab meat. Cut each half in 6 pieces. When ready to use, bake in 350 degree oven for 25 minutes or until browned.

Note: These can be frozen prior to baking.

Wayne C. Anderson

Wayne Anderson is president and chief executive officer of the Arizona Chamber of Commerce. Wayne was the first senior-level nonlawyer executive to be associated with an Arizona law firm and one of the earliest to hold such a position in the United States. He is listed in Who's Who in Arizona, Who's Who in Finance and Industry, Who's Who in Washington, D.C., Who's Who in the East, Who's Who in the West and Who's Who in the World. As a nationally recognized corporate executive with a unique combination of management and public affairs expertise and experience, Wayne has involved himself in many business, government, community and academic endeavors.

MOM'S EGGROLLS

FILLING
3 C. finely ground sirloin
2 C. finely ground pork
3 C. Chinese cabbage (rinsed and squeezed dry, then finely
    chop leaves only, not stalk)
3 C. finely chopped yellow onion
1/2 C. dark soy sauce
2 tsp. minced fresh garlic
2 tsp. grated fresh ginger
dash salt
dash sugar
few drops sesame seed oil

Heat pot of cooking oil for deep frying.

Combine above ingredients in a large bowl and mix well with hands. Beat **one egg** in a small bowl. Lightly brush **store-bought eggroll wrapper** with beaten egg (completely covering wrapper, especially the corners).

Put eggroll meat filling in center of wrapper and roll tightly like a log. Firmly press ends flat to seal (eggroll should look like a pillow).

Set onto tray (seam side up) and let egg harden to seal the eggroll before deep frying. When oil is hot, deep fry about 10 at a time, until golden brown and the meat filling is done. Drain and serve hot. If you like, these eggrolls can be frozen. To re-serve, simply thaw and warm in oven or toaster oven.

Lin Sue Shepherd

Lin Sue Shepherd

Lin Sue Shepherd is news anchor for KPNX, Channel 12 News, in Phoenix.

CRAB DIP

Since Paul was busy coaching the 1993 Western Conference Champion Phoenix Suns, his wife Cindy graciously submitted this winning recipe.

1 1/2 lbs. fresh crab
1 C. freshly grated parmesan cheese
1 C. (or more) chopped scallions
1 jar quartered artichoke hearts, packed in water
1 C. mayonnaise

Mix all ingredients in one bowl. Pour into casserole dish to bake covered in 350 degree oven for 20 minutes. Uncover, sprinkle cheddar cheese on top. Broil to melt. Serve with sturdy crackers.

Paul Westphal

Paul Westphal is the head coach for the Phoenix Suns and is the "winningest" rookie coach in National Basketball Association history with 62 victories his first season. He ranks as the number 4 all-time scorer in Suns' history (9,564 points). Overall, Westphal was a five-time NBA All-Star and was named All-NBA four times. Paul's #44 was retired on 4/15/89, making him the fourth player in Suns' history to have his number retired along with Connie Hawkins #42, Alvan Adams #33 and Dick Van Arsdale #5. Westphal was Cotton Fitzsimmon's assistant coach for the Suns before becoming the head coach July 1, 1992.

SPICY CHILI DIP

1 1/2 lbs. ground beef, crumbled and fried
2 cans cheese soup
1 can (4 oz.) diced green chiles
1 bottle (8 oz.) medium salsa

Fry hamburger, drain. Add remaining ingredients, stir until mixed together and heat thoroughly. Serve warm with tortilla chips. (For the less adventuresome, use mild salsa or for those so inclined, hot salsa will really add some spice.)

Carol Springer

Carol Springer, of Prescott, is an Arizona state senator representing District 1. The 41st Legislature (1993-1994) Directory lists her occupation as real estate broker. Committee assignments are: Appropriations, Chair; Judiciary; Transportation.

GUACAMOLE

2 med. ripe avocados
1 pt. cottage cheese
1 can green chiles, chopped

2 dashes each: salt
and garlic powder
hot sauce

Mash all ingredients together. Add few drops of hot sauce to taste. Serve with tortilla chips. Serving hint: leave pit of avocado in dip to keep it from turning brown.

Alan Stephens

Alan Stephens of Phoenix is a former Arizona state senator who represented District 6. The 40th Legislature (1991-1992) Directory lists his occupation as accountant. Committee assignments were: Appropriations; Government; Health; Natural Resources and Agriculture; Rules.

TABOOLI or SAF-SOOF

"One of my mother's favorite recipes."

1/2 C. wheat, soaked 1/2 hour
3 bunch parsley, stemmed and diced
1 bunch green onions, diced (or 1 dry onion)
small handful of fresh mint, stemmed and diced
4 tomatoes, diced
lettuce or fresh grape leaves

Drain wheat by squeezing out water. Combine with next four ingredients. Season with your choice of herbs and spices and serve on lettuce or grape leaves.

Eddie Basha

Eddie Basha is the chief executive officer of Basha's Food Stores. He was honored as 1989 Phoenix Man of the Year and has served on; Arizona's Board of Regents since 1990; State Board of Education (1982-1990); Chandler School Board (1968-1980); and was the 1987 co-founder of Children's Action Alliance. Eddie is very involved in state and community affairs.

MOGOLLON MOUNTAIN CHILI

2 lbs. ground beef
2 onions, chopped
2 sm. cans diced green chiles
3 bouillon cubes

Brown ground beef and drain off fat. Add remaining ingredients and cook until onions are translucent.

Put above ingredients in large stew pot and add:

1-15 oz. can stewed tomatoes
2 cans kidney beans
4 Tbsp. chili powder
1 Tbsp. garlic powder
1 Tbsp. black pepper
1 Tbsp. ground oregano
1 tsp. celery salt
1 tsp. crushed red pepper
2 Tbsp. sugar

Simmer for 1 hour. Sit back and enjoy!

From the Kitchen of the
Christopher Creek Landmark Cafe

The Christopher Creek Landmark Cafe

The Christopher Creek Landmark Cafe (just north of Payson on highway 260) is famous for its chili. The next time you're up that way, be sure to stop by.

ARIZONA'S FINE CHILI

1 lb. coarse ground beef
2 C. chopped onion
1 can tomato puree (6 oz.)
1 lb. dry pinto beans*

3 Tbsp. chili powder
salt to taste
1 Tbsp. cumin
water

Sauté beef and drain off excess fat. Add onions, puree and beans. Mix chili powder, salt and cumin; add to mixture. Bring to a boil, turn down heat and cook slowly until onions and beans are tender, adding water to desired consistency.

*Beans can be soaked overnight, or if added dry chili must cook long enough for them to become tender.

Yield: Serves 4 to 6 persons.

Barry Goldwater

Barry Goldwater is a former United States Senator from Arizona and former Republican Party nominee for President of the United States. While in the Senate, he served on the Aeronautical and Space Sciences Committee, the Armed Services Committee, the Preparedness Investigating Subcommittee, Tactical Air Power Subcommittee, Intelligence Subcommittee, Military Construction Subcommittee, and the Research and Development Subcommittee. He is the 1949 Phoenix Man of the Year and an internationally recognized photographer.

PAUL HARVEY'S WILD RICE SOUP

"It's the best soup I ever tasted."
Paul Harvey, November 1984

1/2 C. uncooked wild rice
2 Tbsp. butter or margarine
1 med. onion, minced
1 C. water
1 qt. milk
2 cans cream of potato soup
1 lb. Velveeta® cheese
Optional: 10 strips crisp bacon, crumbled (I think
    you'll want to use the bacon)

In separate sauce pan prepare wild rice according to basic recipe. Sauté onion in butter until tender. Add water, milk, and potato soup. Increase heat to medium, stirring occasionally. When mixture is hot, add cheese in chunks to speed melting. When creamy, add cooked wild rice. Garnish with crumbled bacon.

For variations, sauté mushrooms and/or green pepper with onion.

Yield: Serves 6 to 8.

Note: This soup can burn easily on the bottom, especially when reheating, if it is not stirred often enough or heat is too high. Burnt wild rice soup is not the best - we know from experience. This soup actually tastes better the next day.

Jan Brewer

Janice Kay Brewer

Jan Brewer of Glendale is the Arizona state senator representing District 19. The 41st Arizona Legislature (1993-1994) Directory lists her occupation as businesswoman. Committee assignments are: Rules, Vice Chair; Commerce and Economic Development; Health, Welfare and Aging.

MEXICAN FRITO SOUP

Sauté for five minutes the following:

2 sm. onions, chopped
2 cans diced green chiles
4 cloves crushed garlic
4 Tbsp. vegetable oil

Then add:

2 lg. chopped tomatoes
2 tsp. salt
2 cans beef broth
4 tsp. Worcestershire sauce
2 cans chicken broth
8 pre-boiled chicken breasts, cut in bite sizes
3 C. water
2 med. cans of sweet white corn, drained
3 C. tomato juice
2 tsp. chili powder
2 tsp. cumin

Bring to a boil. Add **1/4 cup barley** and simmer for one hour. Serve soup in bowls, leaving room for guests to add any or all of the following garnishes: grated cheese, chopped green onions, sour cream, **Frito® corn chips**.

Yield: 8 to 10.

David Ira Goldstein

David Ira Goldstein is in his first season as artistic director of The Arizona Theatre Company. He comes to Arizona from Seattle and has guest-directed at theatres across the country. His production of George Sand's *Minnesota* traveled to the Edinburgh International Festival in Scotland, and his production of *Sea Marks* toured Alaska. He was a co-founder of Minnesota Young Playwrights and has served as an on-site reporter for the National Endowment for the Arts for the past seven years.

HAZELWOOD'S SIMPLY ELEGANT CHICKEN SOUP

2 chicken breasts, skinned, deboned, and cut into cubes
juice of 1 lemon
salt and pepper
4 C. chicken broth
1 sm. bunch cilantro, washed and chopped
2 green onions, green stem only, chopped
1/2 lg. tomato, chopped
1/2 tsp. salt
1 avocado, chopped and sprinkled with lemon juice
2 carrots, shredded
1/2 C. frozen tender peas, thawed

Sprinkle chicken with juice of one lemon, salt and pepper to taste. Marinate for 15 minutes. Prepare all other vegetables. Heat broth and hold on low heat. Put chicken in microwave-save casserole and cover loosely with plastic wrap. Microwave on High for 2 minutes. Stir chicken and microwave 1 1/2 minutes more. Let steam settle before uncovering. Lightly mix cilantro, green onion and tomato. Add salt and avocado and gently toss. Divide into 4 large serving bowls. Top with 1/4 carrot and 2 tablespoons peas. Place 1/4 of the cubed chicken breast pieces on top of each mound of vegetables. Pour 1 cup of simmering chicken broth into each bowl. Serve immediately with corn chips on the side.

Richard L. Hazelwood

Rich Hazelwood is the president of Hazelwood Enterprises Inc. in Tempe which designs and produces a wide variety of silk-screen T-shirts. Hazelwood provides $20,000 annually to be used for cash awards to the outstanding teacher, principal and pupils in the Creighton Elementary School District. He believes that it is particularly important that small businesses actively support education, because many of the people they hire will be the products of the local schools. He has also been involved with two Junior Achievement programs in the district.

GLEN'S FAVORITE CHILI

1/2 lb. dry pinto beans
5 cups canned tomatoes, peeled
1 lb. green bell peppers, seeded
    and coarsly chopped
1 1/2 lbs. onions, peeled and
    coarsly chopped
2 cloves garlic, crushed
1 1/2 tbsp. olive oil

1/2 C. minced parsley
1 1/2 lbs. hamburger meat
1 lb. ground lean pork
1/3 cup chili powder
2 Tbsp. salt
1 1/2 tsp. pepper
1 1/2 tsp. cumin seed

Soak pinto beans overnight in cold water in large chili pot. Cover beans with fresh cold water and simmer for two hours. Sauté green bell peppers, onions, garlic, and parsley in olive oil. Brown pork and hamburger, add spices and cook for ten minutes. Combine with beans and cook covered for one hour. Uncover and cook for another 30 minutes. (Add water if needed). Makes 4 quarts of chili.

Glen Campbell

Glen Campbell is one of those rare artists who was able to take country music into the mainstream. Glen enjoyed incredible success with early hits such as *Gentle On My Mind, By the Time I Get to Phoenix, Wichita Lineman* and *Galveston.* He also scored with *Rhinestone Cowboy* and *Southern Nights.* He has won Grammy Awards and been named Male Vocalist of the Year. Glen lives in the Valley and still produces beautiful music. His newest album is *Somebody Like That.* Glen is an active participant in celebrity golf tournaments which benefit numerous charitable organizations in the Valley.

FIT FOR A QUEEN STEW

6 med. potatoes, chunked
6 to 8 carrots, chunked
3 to 4 celery stalks, chunked
3 sm. onions, chunked
2 cans stewed tomatoes
2 Tbsp. grape jelly
1 Tbsp. minced garlic
1/2 C. red wine
2 to 2 1/4 lb. stew meat
3/4 Tbsp. Lawry's® seasoning salt
3/4 Tbsp. black pepper
3 Tbsp. tapioca

Place first 8 ingredients in large roaster. Spread meat, seasonings and tapioca on top. Cover tightly. Roast 4 hours at 275 degrees. Stir and serve.

Vonda Van Dyke

Vonda Van Dyke is a former Miss Arizona and was crowned Miss America, 1965. She now resides in Minnesota.

BEEF STEW

(Made in Microwave)

4 Tbsp. vegetable oil	1 lg. onion, chopped
1/4 C. flour	1 green pepper, diced
salt and pepper	3 med. carrots,
2 lbs. boneless lean beef chuck, cut into 1-inch cubes	6 med. potatoes
2 1/2 C. water	2 stalks celery
2 bay leaves	3 ripe tomatoes, diced
2 tsp. salt	1/2 C. catsup
1/4 tsp. pepper	3 to 6 Tbsp. flour
1 clove garlic	3/4 C. cold water
	1 (10 oz.) pkg. frozen peas

Heat 2 tablespoons of oil in large skillet over moderate heat on conventional range. Combine flour, salt, pepper to taste in a plastic bag. Shake meat cubes in seasoned flour to coat. Brown beef cubes, a few at a time, on all sides in hot oil. Add the remaining 2 tablespoons of oil as needed. Transfer browned beef cubes into a deep, 3-quart, heat-resistant, non-metallic casserole. Add 2 1/2 cups water, bay leaves, 2 teaspoons salt, 1/4 teaspoon pepper and peeled and crushed garlic. Heat, uncovered, on simmer for 15 minutes. Stir once. Skim any foam that may form.

Add onions and green peppers to skillet and brown slightly. Add onion, green peppers, carrots and potatoes (peeled and cubed), celery (cut in 1/2" slices) and catsup to casserole. Stir to combine. Heat, covered, on simmer for 1 hour or until meat and vegetables are tender. While beef and vegetables are cooking, combine the 6 tablespoons flour and the 3/4 cup of water in small bowl. Remove bay leaves, if desired, from stew. Once all ingredients are tender, gradually stir the flour mixture into the stew. If desired, add **1/2 to 1 tsp. brown bouquet sauce**, a little at a time until desired color is reached. Color will deepen as stew cooks. Add partially thawed peas and heat, covered, on simmer for 10-15 minutes, or until sauce is thickened and peas are hot.

Herbert E. Osman

Herbert E. Osman

Herb Osman is the senior pastor at Red Mountain United Methodist Church in Mesa. Herb serves on a multitude of civic boards and concentrates his energies on addressing the needs of the homeless.

MOOSEHEAD STEW

1 1/2 lb. Polish kielbasa
1 onion
1 lg. clove garlic
6 potatoes, diced
6 carrots, diced
2 bottles Moosehead® beer
2 tsp. Lawry's® seasoned pepper
1 sm. white cabbage

Brown sausage, onion and thinly sliced garlic. Add potatoes and carrots and pour in the two bottles of beer. Dust with pepper. Simmer one hour, last 15 minutes add cabbage, cut into small wedges, to steam on top of stew.

Yiold: For four big caters!

Dick Arentz

Dick Arentz is a photographer and platinum/paladium printer. Dick has had 50 one-man exhibits in the United States and Europe in most major museum collections including The New York and San Francisco museums of modern art, The George Eastman House, Corcoran Gallery and The Center for Creative Photography. In 1978, he was selected by the Arts and Humanities Commission as one of the "Twenty Arizona Artists".

CHAMPIGNONS AUF WHALEN
(Mushroom Gravy)

1 lb. mushrooms, fresh	2 C. red wine
1 can (14 1/2 oz.) beef	1 Tbsp. sweet vermouth
broth, clear	1 tsp. Worcestershire sauce
pepper	2 Tbsp. soy sauce
3 bacon slices, thick	bitters
2 lg. garlic cloves	corn starch, flour or
3 shallots	arrowroot
1 sm. onion	

Clean mushrooms. Separate caps and stems. Place beef broth (undiluted) in large saucepan. Add dash of ground pepper and bring to simmer. Fry bacon in cast iron skillet until quite crisp. Remove bacon and crumble. Add to beef broth. Reserve bacon fat in skillet.

Mince garlic. Slice mushroom stems, shallots and onion thin and sauté in bacon fat until well done. Add to beef broth. Reserve 2 tablespoons bacon fat.

Combine wine, vermouth, Worcestershire and soy sauces. Add dash of bitters. Deglaze skillet, bringing liquid to boil. Add liquid to beef broth mixture. Simmer for 1 hour.

Lightly brown mushroom caps in skillet using reserved bacon fat. Add mushroom caps to beef broth mixture. Simmer for 10 minutes. Thicken with roux or a mixture of water and corn starch, flour or arrowroot, to taste.

Martin J. Whalen

Marty Whalen is an aviation lawyer who serves as senior vice president and general counsel for America West Airlines. He and Mary-Jo, his spouse of 29 years, moved to Mesa in 1986 and both are active in community civic and charitable endeavors. The Whalens are ardent Superstition Mountain hikers and explorers of back-country Arizona. The two like to cook together and are given to occasional bouts of culinary experimentation. This interest reached a milestone of sorts when, after three days in the kitchen, an authentic, mouth-watering cassoulet, done from scratch, was summarily written off as "Oh, pork and beans..." by a neighbor who had been brought up in Paris.

VEGETABLE SOUP

1 (6 lb.) beef brisket
1 pkg. Knox® oxtail soup mix
1 can (28 oz.) tomatoes
6 C. water
1 med. onion, chopped
any fresh vegetables cut into bite sizes

Combine all ingredients except vegetables, bring to boil and simmer 2 1/2 hours. Remove brisket and place in separate pan. Spoon 1/2 cup broth over it, cover with foil and chill. Chill broth and beef until 1 1/2 hours before serving. Spoon off hardened grease and reheat broth. Heat covered beef in 325 degree oven for 30 minutes. Drop in vegetables and serve when tender with onion toast. Thinly slice beef against the grain and serve on a separate platter with horseradish sauce.

Yield: 10 servings.

Nancy Berge

Nancy Berge

Nancy Berge is editor for the cookbook "*Con Mucho Gusto*" which was a project she chaired for the Desert Club in Mesa. She noted that the beauty of these recipes is that they can be prepared a day in advance for an upcoming event or entertaining. Nancy is a native of Arizona, and was a teacher in Mesa and Scottsdale. Her days are now filled with various volunteer efforts for some of her favorite charities. Nancy served on the founding board for the Arizona Museum for Youth, the Mesa Educational Foundation Board, the Mesa Symphony Music Guild and is a member of the Desert Club in Mesa. She also presently serves on the Major Gifts committee for the University of Arizona and the Advisory Board to the College of Education for the University of Arizona where she received her B.A. in Education. She received her M.A. in Education from Arizona State University.

STARGAZER'S CHILI

1/2 lb. ground chuck
2 Tbsp. chopped onion
1 can pinto beans
1 Tbsp. chili powder
1 sm. can chopped green chile peppers
1 can tomatoes
salt to taste

Brown meat in iron skillet. Drain grease and add other ingredients. Simmer for 20 minutes. Serve with corn bread.

Robert L. Millis

Robert Millis is the director for Lowell Observatory on Mars Hill Road in Flagstaff. He began his experience there as staff astronomer in 1967. He is currently a member of the board of editors, Publications of the Astronomical Society of the Pacific, and chairman, Scientific Organizing Committee, 106th annual meeting, "Completing the Inventory of the Solar System," Flagstaff, June 1994. He has also served on several NASA teams and panels.

CINCINNATI CHILI

1 1/2 lb. lean ground sirloin
sm. onion, chopped
1 - 20 oz. can tomato sauce
1 - 14 oz. can peeled whole tomatoes
1/2 tsp. cinnamon
1/2 tsp. allspice
1 tsp. salt
1/2 tsp. pepper
1 1/2 Tbsp. chili powder
1 Tbsp. vinegar
1 clove garlic
3 bay leaves

Brown meat with chopped onions. Drain grease. Place meat and onions in large pan or crock pot with all other ingredients. Cook slowly 4 to 5 hours, covered. Remove bay leaves and garlic before serving. Serve over bed of spaghetti, topped with grated cheddar cheese.

Yield: Serves 6 - 8.

Jeffrey C. Bruce

Jeff Bruce is the executive editor of the Tribune Newspapers serving Mesa, Chandler, Tempe, Gilbert and Scottsdale. He chose this recipe because he grew up in New Haven, Ohio — a small town outside Cincinnati — where some of his fondest childhood memories are of driving to the big city to watch the Cincinnati Redlegs play baseball at the old Crosley Field , and eating chili with his dad after the games. (Author's note: Jeff is also my best friend, the father of my children, and the best husband a woman could ever have!)

LATTIE'S HOT CHILI

2 Tbsp. oil
2 med. onions, chopped
4 cloves garlic, chopped
1 lg. green pepper, chopped
1 lb. ground beef
4 - 16 oz. cans whole tomatoes
1 - 12 oz. can tomato paste

4 - 16 oz. cans kidney beans
2 C. water
1 1/2 Tbsp. salt
1/2 tsp. crushed red pepper
3 - 4 tsp. chili powder
   (more or less to taste)
Tabasco® sauce, optional

Heat oil in large pot. Add onion, garlic and green pepper and sauté until crisp-tender. Remove sautéed vegetables. Add ground beef and cook until well browned, stirring frequently. Add additional oil if necessary.

Add sautéed vegetables to meat along with remaining ingredients, bringing to a boil. Reduce heat and simmer over low heat 3 to 4 hours, stirring frequently to prevent burning. Taste after 2 hours and season with additional chili, Tabasco, salt and pepper.

Yield: Makes 16 cups.

Lattie F. Coor

Lattie Coor is the president of Arizona State University.

FRUIT, FRUIT AND MORE FRUIT!

"A great dish for humans, too!"

3 lg. lettuce leaves
1 banana
3 cherries (with stems)
10 grapes (green and red)
1 apple
1 orange
5 canteloupe balls

Carefully wash the lettuce leaves and place on a plate. Cut the banana in half, place in the center of the plate and top with a cherry. Wash and slice all the other ingredients in bite sizes and arrange on the plate in a colorful assortment.

Ric Adams for Alex

Alex is a male Gibbon Ape. He comes from the jungles of Southeast Asia and was adopted by human parents (Lee and Ric Adams) from a zoo in Arizona in 1990. You might have caught a glimpse of Alex at a celebrity gig, one of his latest being with Apryl Hettich, Miss Arizona USA 1993. Alex's mom, Lee, also raises Bengal Cats. Sounds like Alex is a very lucky guy to have such swell parents who really enjoy living in an *"Animal House"*.

AVOCADO - GRAPEFRUIT SALAD

2 to 3 heads Bibb lettuce, washed, drained, torn into bite size
2 ripe avocados, sliced just before serving
2 to 3 grapefruits, sectioned, juice drained

DRESSING
1/2 C. sugar
1 tsp. dry mustard
1 1/2 tsp. celery salt
1 tsp. paprika

1 tsp. grated onion
1 C. salad oil
1/4 C. vinegar (red wine)

Mix dressing. Arrange lettuce, avocado slices and grapefruit sections on cool salad plates, top with dressing.

Debbie Bryant Berge

Debbie Bryant Berge

Debbie Berge, formerly Miss Kansas, was crowned Miss America in 1966. She now resides in Arizona.

GINGER CHICKEN SALAD

1- 6 oz. package long grain
**   and wild rice mix**
2 C. cooked shredded
**   chicken breast**
1/2 C. sliced green onions

4 plums, sliced
2 Tbsp. oil
2 Tbsp. lemon juice
1 Tbsp. soy sauce
1/2 tsp. ginger

Prepare rice mix as directed and cool. Combine rice, chicken, onions, and plums. To prepare dressing, combine remaining ingredients in separate bowl and toss lightly with rice mixture. Cover and chill. Yield: 6 servings.

Kathy Alexander

Kathy Alexander

Kathy is the vice president/ director of the University of Phoenix in Tucson. She also is the author of *Paradise Found: The Settlement of the Santa Catalina Mountains*.

TACO SALAD

1 head lettuce, finely
    chopped
1/2 lb. ground sirloin of beef
1 lg. tomatoe, diced

1 1/2 cups grated cheddar
    cheese
3/4 C. your favorite dressing
3 Tbsp. sour cream

Wash and chop lettuce in advance. Place lettuce in a colander so that all moisture can drip out of the lettuce before preparing the salad. Place colander in the refrigerator. Crumble the ground sirloin and cook over medium heat until just done (drain fat).

Put the chopped lettuce, diced tomatoes, cooked warm sirloin and 3/4 cup of the grated cheddar cheese in a large mixing bowl. Add your favorite dressing and toss well. Divide the salad on 6 plates. Sprinkle remaining 3/4 cups of grated cheddar cheese evenly on the top of each serving. Put 1 1/2 teaspoons sour cream on top of each salad. I like to serve this with toasted tortilla triangles.

Erma Bombeck

Erma Bombeck

Erma Bombeck is a nationally syndicated newspaper columnist. The 1986 Phoenix Woman of the Year honoree was also honored recently for her contributions to the American Cancer Society, which received $1 million in U.S. royalties from a book she wrote— *I Want to Grow Hair, I Want to Grow Up, I Want to Go to Boise* —about children surviving cancer. $500,000 from the book royalties outside the United States also were donated by Erma and her husband, Bill Bombeck, to the Eleanor Roosevelt International Cancer Research Fellowships.

TURKEY SALAD

2 C. diced, cooked turkey
1/2 C. diced celery
1 sm. zucchini, chopped
1/2 red bell pepper, chopped
2 Tbsp. sweet pickle relish
1 C. shredded lettuce

Place turkey in a bowl large enough to hold all ingredients. Add celery, zucchini, red pepper and relish and mix well. Add lettuce and toss to mix. Stir in enough Buttermilk Dressing (or your favorite dressing) to coat salad ingredients. May be served as a main dish salad or stuffed into pita bread halves.

Yield: Serves 6.

Buttermilk Dressing

3/4 C. mayonnaise
3/4 C. buttermilk
1/8 tsp. black pepper
1 tsp. dried minced garlic
1/2 tsp. celery salt

Combine all ingredients, in order given, in a pint jar. Shake vigorously until mixed. Make at least two hours ahead of time to allow flavors to blend. Store in refrigerator.

Ferne Holmes

Ferne Holmes

Ferne Holmes writes a monthly cooking column for *Arizona Hunter & Angler* magazine and does free lance work for several other outdoor publications. Her two books *Easy Recipes for Wild Game and Fish* and *Easy Recipes for the Traveling Cook* are popular throughout the Southwest.

SOUR CREAM FRUIT SALAD

1 - 16 oz. can pineapple, crushed and drained
8 to 10 bananas, diced
1 1/2 C. miniature marshmallows (optional)
1 - 8 oz. package frozen sweetened strawberries (thawed
    and drained)
1/2 C. chopped pecans or walnuts
1/2 C. sugar
2 Tbsp. lemon juice
1 - 16 oz. carton sour cream or non-fat vanilla yogurt

Mix all ingredients and chill 2 hours.

Farrell Jensen

Farrell Jensen is a city council member for the city of Mesa.

SCUNGILLI SALAD

Toss together: **Chilled Scungilli (6 to 8 oz. can), sliced garlic** to taste, season to taste with **salt, pepper,** and **parsley.** Add approximately **2 tablespoons olive oil** and squeeze about **1/3 of a medium lemon** over mixture. Toss and serve cold with hot Italian bread.

Danielle Ammaccapane

Danielle Ammaccapane is one of Arizona's LPGA members. She won three tournaments in 1992—the Standard Register Ping, Centel Classic and Lady Keystone Open. She has one other career victory, the 1991 Standard Register Ping. She attended Arizona State University. *"When I come home from the tour, this is one of my favorite dishes my father makes for me at the restaurant."* Her father, Ralph, owns Ammaccapane's, a sports bar and restaurant in Phoenix.

CAESAR SALAD

Salt bottom of wooden salad bowl and add:

4 lg. garlic cloves, peeled and pressed
2 fillets of anchovy per person, split
grating of black pepper

Work to a paste then add:

juice of one lemon
2 to 3 Tbsp. of Worcestershire sauce
3 to 3 1/2 tsp. Grey Poupon® mustard

Work into bowl adding **coarse pepper** to taste. Mixing with vigor, shake on sides of bowl: **1 part olive oil to 1/3 vinegar.** Add **2 heads romaine lettuce** broken to 2-inch lengths.

Cook **one egg** gently in simmering water for 1 to 1 1/2 minutes. Drop the egg from the shell into the ingredients in the bowl, add **croutons** and 2 to 3 tablespoons of **Parmesan cheese.** Toss the salad well. Serve at once. Yield: 4 servings.

Lynda Carter

Lynda Carter, a native of Phoenix, is a well-known actress and former Miss World USA 1970. Her first acting break which launched her career, came when she was cast as the star of the television series *"Wonder Woman"*, which ran for five years beginning in 1976. She is deeply involved in charities benefiting children and also charitable causes like the Susan G. Komen Foundation (for breast cancer education and research) for which she received the Jill Ireland Award for Volunteerism.

CHINESE CHICKEN SALAD

1/2 to 3/4 lb. chicken breast, white meat, cooked and shredded
1 package maifun noodles ("rice sticks"), deep fried
1 head lettuce, shredded fine
4 to 5 green onions, sliced fine
1 Tbsp. sesame seeds, optional

Boil chicken in chicken broth until done, or salt and pepper breast, seal in foil and bake 45 minutes or until cooked. Let cool, shred, or if pressed for time, slice in thin strips. Deep fry noodles in about 3" of oil, drain well on paper towels. Do not refrigerate. Keep in dry place. If noodles become limp, crisp them in 250 degree oven between paper towels on a roasting pan for 10 minutes.

DRESSING: Mix in wide-mouth jar, shake well, pour on lightly just before serving.

4 Tbsp. sugar	**1/2 C. salad oil**
2 tsp. salt	**2 Tbsp. sesame seed oil**
2 tsp. Accent®	**6 Tbsp. white vinegar**
1 tsp. black pepper	

To serve: In large bowl, add 1/2 of lettuce, onions, chicken and noodles. Pour on dressing. Toss lightly.

Note: This is a large recipe, so mix 1/2 batch at a time to keep it from going limp. Also, about 3/4 of the package of noodles is sufficient for one head of lettuce.

Jim Kolbe

Jim Kolbe

Jim Kolbe is a U. S. Congressman, serving in District 5. He was elected to the Arizona State Senate 1976, 1978, and 1980. He was elected to the U. S. House of Representatives in 1984. The congressman has served as: director of Vietnam Orphan Airlift, 1975; Board of Directors: Job Bank; Casa De Los Ninos; Community Food Bank.

TURKEY GINGER SALAD

DRESSING
1/2 C. white vinegar
1 C. sugar
2 1/2 tsp. ground ginger
1 tsp. salt

Heat until sugar is dissolved. Put in mixer. Beat on low, gradually adding:
1 1/2 C. salad oil

Beat on high until well blended. Stir in:
3 Tbsp. sesame seeds

TOPPING
1 lb. sliced turkey, cut into approximate 1-inch squares
    (cooked breast is best)
3 Tbsp. soy sauce
2 Tbsp. salad oil
2 med. cloves fresh garlic, minced

Place in frying pan and saute until all liquid is gone and meat is hot. Set aside to cool. Chill.
2 med. tomatoes, cubed
4 stalks celery, diced
4 oz. dressing

Mix with chilled meat mixture.

Divide salad topping into 4 to 6 equal portions, depending on the size salad you want. Spread over the top of 2 to 3 cups chopped lettuce, add additional dressing as desired. Enjoy!

H.M. (Butch) Opsahl

Butch Opsahl is president of the Yuma County Chamber of Commerce.

GINGER & TARRAGON DRESSING

1 sm. finely chopped onion
1 C. and 2 Tbsp. olive oil
1 tsp. garlic paste
1 C. chicken or vegetable broth

1/2 C. vinegar
1 Tbsp. ground ginger
2 Tbsp. tarragon

Gently soften onion in 2 tablespoons olive oil and add garlic paste. Add broth and boil for five minutes. Add 1/4 cup vinegar, mix well and continue boiling for 2 minutes. Remove from heat and allow to cool while you make a vinaigrette by (furiously) whisking a further 1/4 cup of the vinegar with 1 cup of olive oil; add this to the mixture and stir in. If you choose to use dried herbs, add a good tablespoon of ground ginger and 2 tablespoons of tarragon, and shake vigorously. If you have the fresh herbs, triple the quantity; chop the tarragon finely and grate the ginger.

Alan Caillou

Alan Caillou, who now lives in Arizona, was born in England in 1914 and trained as an actor at the Oscar Lewis Academy. In 1934, he went to Palestine and served in the Palestine Police, traveling between Palestine, Egypt, the Sudan, Lebanon, Syria and the Trans-Jordan. At the outbreak of World War II, he joined the British Army's Intelligence Corps. He was captured and court-martialled on charges of espionage, sentenced to be shot but escaped. He was recaptured and escaped on several occasions, and he spent the remainder of the war with the guerrillas in Yugoslavia and Italy as Intelligence Officer to the Partisan Ninth Corps. At the end of the hostilities in Europe he was sent to Ethiopia to take over the administration of the Reserved Areas Police and became the Chief of Police in Dire Dawa. Later, he had a "one-man" station in unexplored territory in Somalia. He was constantly on safari over 10,000 square miles inhabited by a dozen warring tribes. In 1948, he became a civilian and took up his old profession — writing and acting. He has written thirty-five books, which have been translated into ten different languages. Caillou has written twelve motion pictures. He acted in twenty-one movies as well as scores of television plays. *The World is Six Feet Square* is an autobiography about his life in prison; another *Sheba Slept Here* is also autobiographical, concerning his years as chief of police in Ethiopia.

24 HOUR SLAW

Combine in a large salad bowl:
1 lg. head cabbage, chopped rather coarsely
1 sm. onion, chopped
1 green pepper, sliced
12 stuffed olives (or more), sliced
1 carrot, grated
1 or 2 stalks celery, chopped
  DRESSING
1/2 C. water
2 C. sugar
1 C. white vinegar
1/2 tsp. celery seed
1/2 tsp. dry mustard
1 Tbsp. salt

Boil dressing gently for 15 minutes. Pour hot dressing over vegetables. Cool and refrigerate 24 hours or more. To serve, use slotted spoon or drain. This will keep a week or more.

Nancy Wessel

Nancy Wessel of Phoenix. is a retired member of the Arizona House of Representatives serving District 19. The 41st Arizona Legislature (1993-1994) Directory lists her occupation as legislator/homemaker. Committee assignments were: Health, Chair; Rules.

GERMAN HOT POTATO SALAD

8 med. red potatoes
1/2 lb. bacon
1/4 C. sliced green olives
1/2 C. diced onions
1/2 C. chopped celery
1/2 chopped green pepper
2 eggs, beaten
4 eggs, hard boiled and diced
3/4 C. vinegar
1/4 C. water
1 Tbsp. sugar
3 Tbsp. salt
1/4 tsp. paprika
3/4 tsp. dry mustard
1/4 tsp. pepper

Cook potatoes, peel, slice thinly while hot. Fry bacon crisp and crumble. Add olives, onions, celery, green pepper to 2 tablespoons bacon fat. Sauté. Heat to boiling: vinegar, water, sugar, salt, paprika, mustard and pepper. Beat eggs, add onion and vinegar mixtures. Layer potatoes, bacon and crumbled hard boiled eggs in large frying pan. Pour egg mixture over top, beat and stir gently.

Serve warm.

Diana Smith

Diana Smith

Diana Smith is the publisher and owner of the *Scottsdale Airpark News*. She is also past chairman of Scottsdale Leadership (1991-1992). She wrote, "For many years, my husband, Dave, and I, with our 2 daughters, moved and lived in many different parts of the country.(15 places in 20 years). We created this recipe from the best of all the German potato salad recipes we enjoyed. Hopefully, you will find a bit of the south, east and midwest in it."

CABBAGE-PEANUT SLAW SALAD

SLAW
1 lg. head cabbage
1 12-oz. can salted Spanish peanuts
DRESSING
2/3 C. sour cream
2/3 C. mayonnaise
4 tsp. lemon juice
4 tsp. sugar

Trim, quarter and finely shred cabbage (approximately 10 cups). Set aside. Combine ingredients for dressing and mix well. Before serving, combine cabbage and dressing and mix well. Add peanuts (reserve 1/4 cup) and gently stir until evenly distributed. Sprinkle reserved peanuts on top.

Ivan W. Reece

Ivan Reece is a sculptor who creates figures from pieces of egg cartons. He is a retired school teacher who calls his handywork REECE'S RECESS! He even has do-it-yourself kits for the little ones to make ducks and things. (Author's note: Ivan's recipe is one of the recipes I have used about a dozen times lately at different gatherings because it is so easy and really tasty. Everyone always asks me about the slaw and I tell them about Ivan's egg cartons. I was pleasantly surprised at the number of people who already knew about Ivan's sculptures. He is a very popular guy with a talent unmatched by any other and just think—he's recycling, too!)

HOT CHICKEN SALAD

Mix together:

4 C. cooked chicken

1 1/2 C. finely diced celery

1 C. water chestnuts (sliced)

Mix and add:

1 C. mayonnaise

1 can cream of mushroom soup

Pour into buttered casserole and top with **1 package Pepperidge Farms® cornbread stuffing mix,** mixed with **3/4 cups melted margarine.** Bake at 350 degrees for 1 hour.

Yield: Serves 8.

Robert Luther "Lute" Olson

Lute Olson is the men's head basketball coach for the University of Arizona in Tucson. Under Coach Olson the Wildcats have been ranked in the Top 20 for five seasons with a 1988 National Collegiate Athletic Association Final Four trip as well. Olson boasts scores of awards including CBS-TV National Coach of the Year 1989, NABC National Coach of the Year 1980, USA Coach for 1986 World Championship titlists, USA Coach for 1984 Jones Cup Champions, 1979 & 1981 Big Ten Coach of the Year to mention only a few. He has U.S. Olympic Players Selection Committee experience and has been a United Press International coaches poll panelist as well as an international and national clinic panelist. Coach Olson helps raise millions for United Way and arthritis research.

QUICK & EASY CAESAR SALAD

(by JoAnn Fitzsimmons)

2 heads romaine lettuce (torn into bite-size pieces)

DRESSING
6 Tbsp. olive oil
1 Tbsp. Worcestershire sauce
1/4 tsp. pepper
1/2 tsp. salt
3 1/2 Tbsp. lemon juice

Shake well. Pour over greens and toss. Add **1/2 cup Parmesan cheese**. Add **croutons**.

Cotton Fitzsimmons

Cotton Fitzsimmons is the senior executive vice president for the Phoenix Suns basketball team. Fitzsimmons assists the Suns' president and chief executive officer, Jerry Colangelo, with the day-to-day operations of the team and is the Suns' television commentator. The former Suns' head coach has an impressive 19-year National Basketball Association coaching record. He boasts the highest percentage winning record of any Suns' coach and on March 31, 1992, he became only the sixth man in NBA history to reach his 800th coaching victory. During Fitzsimmons first year of his second stint with the Suns (in 1988-89), he led the team to win 27 more games than the previous year, which at the time was the third-biggest turnaround in NBA history. The 55-27 record was the second best mark in franchise history, and he was honored as Coach of the Year by the NBA, The Sporting News and Basketball Weekly. Fitzsimmons was inducted into the Missouri Basketball Hall of Fame in 1988 and into the National Junior College Hall of Fame in 1985. He was born in Hannibal, Missouri, and he and his wife JoAnn reside in Phoenix. He enjoys golf and fishing in his spare time.

MEXICAN CASSEROLE SALAD

1 lb. lean ground beef
1/2 med. onion, chopped
1 can chili with beans
1 med. bag Fritos®
1/2 head lettuce, chopped
1 lg. tomato, chopped
1 ripe avocado, cut up
1 can black olives
1 C. grated sharp cheddar cheese
3/4 C. salsa

Brown ground beef and onion. Add can of chili, stir and heat. Spread Fritos on bottom of casserole dish. Spread meat mixture on top of Fritos. Layer with lettuce, tomato, avocado, olives. Cover with grated cheese. Dot with salsa. Place under broiler just until cheese melts. Serve immediately.

Culver "Bill" Nelson

Bill Nelson is presently the executive dean at Western International University and visiting professor at the Pacific School of Religion in Berkeley, California. He was founding pastor in 1954 and later the senior minister of the Church of the Beatitudes, United Church of Christ, Phoenix, until his retirement in 1991. With over 3,000 members, the church became the largest active congregation in its denomination by its 25th year. He received the Freedom Foundation Award twice: for a sermon following the assassination of President John Kennedy and included in the book *That Day With God;* and for a sermon on the Bicentennial of the United States. For 12 years, he was a regular columnist for the *Arizona Republic* and has a recent biography published by the Arizona State University Libraries.

LEAH'S CHICKEN SALAD

4 C. diced cooked chicken
1/2 C. barbecued almonds, chopped
2 C. diced celery
Juice of 1 large lemon
1 1/2 C. real mayonnaise
1/2 lb. bacon, fried crisp

Toss together and serve on lettuce leaf.

Danny White

Danny White is the head coach and general manager for the Arizona Rattlers. Danny is a former quarterback for the Dallas Cowboys. He recently was inducted into the Mesa City Sports Hall of Fame and was honored for his outstanding performance in sports at Westwood High School in 1970.

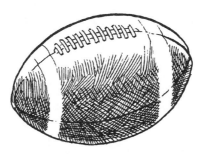

SUMMER SALSA

1 lg. ripe tomato, cored, seeded
    and diced (with any juice)
2 Tbsp. minced cilantro
1 Tbsp. minced chives
1 jalapeño pepper, cored,
    seeded and minced
1 sm. celery stalk, diced
1 Tbsp. olive oil
1 tsp. red wine vinegar
Salt and freshly ground
    white pepper

Combine tomato, cilantro, chives, jalapeño pepper, celery, olive oil, vinegar and salt and pepper to taste in glass or ceramic bowl. Let sit a few minutes for flavors to blend.

Note: Leftovers will keep several hours from lunch to dinner time at room temperature and longer if refrigerated.

Yield: Approximately 1 cup.

Richard F. Archer

Richard Archer is the mayor of Sierra Vista.

CRANBERRY RELISH

1 can whole berry cranberry sauce
1 can mandarin oranges drained
1 can pineapple tidbits drained
1 can pie sliced apples (not apple pie filling)

In a large bowl, mix all together very gently with a wooden spoon. Put in covered container in refrigerator, at least overnight. Will keep one to two weeks.

Corrine C. Brooks

Corrine C. Brooks is involved with United Way, is a board member for the Arizona Museum for Youth Friends and participates in many other community services. (Author's note: This recipe is very dear to me because it is a permanent fixture in my home. Former Mayor Peggy Rubach previously owned our home and had an addition added onto the house. She had many of her friends make tiles that are on the counter tops in the addition. Corrine's Cranberry Relish is on one of the tiles made personally by Corrine. A very special addition indeed!)

POP'S SALSA FRESCA

6 tomatillos (wash and remove outside flaky coating)
6 nice med. tomatoes
2 bunches of green onions
1 fresh jalapeño (very optional)
2 lg. (7 oz.) cans diced green chiles or 2 cups fresh, diced,
     roasted, and peeled
1 bundle fresh cilantro
1/4 C. oil
2 Tbsp. vinegar
salt
pepper
1/2 tsp. oregano

Dice all the ingredients adding to a big bowl as you go. Add the oil, vinegar and spices at the end (to taste) and stir. Stores well in a covered bowl or large jar in refrigerator.

Pat Gilbert

Pat Gilbert

Pat Gilbert is a city councilman for the city of Mesa. *"This is one of my Dad's favorite Sunday afternoon activities and generally accompanies a family gathering, football game, and conversation, often all going on at once. It takes a patient person to dice all the stuff carefully but the results are well worth it! The salsa makes a great dip or sauce. Try it on baked chicken, pork chops, grilled hamburgers, and it is essential for Mexican beef steak. There must be a certain reverence for the labor for the fullest enjoyment of the food!!"*

CRANBERRY SALSA

2 med. red bell peppers, roasted, peeled, seeded
    and cut into 1" pieces
1 C. fresh cranberries, rinsed and drained
1 green onion cut into 1" pieces
1/2 (or more) minced fresh jalapeño pepper
3 Tbsp. cilantro leaves
1 Tbsp. orange juice
zest of 1/2 lime

Chop all ingredients in food processor until coarsely chopped. Then add **1/4 cup of sugar** (or more if desired) and **1/2 teaspoon salt**. This stuff is great with all kinds of meats, not just turkey!

Emily Long

Emily Long

Emily Long is a found-object and ceramic artist. Bottle caps, tin cans, bones, bangles and beads are some of Emily's found treasures that she displays in her creations. *"As an artist, I enjoy the luxury of following my imagination and feeding it with all the images and issues which surround me. I explore careful connections, manipulation, liveliness, mystery and sensuousness of surface to create a dialogue for my fascination with the human soul. People think my work is all fun and games — because that is how I often present it — they don't see that I'm actually dealing with deeper issues. Art doesn't have to hit you in the face — it's better when it causes the viewer to look closely and find the mystery in it."* Emily Long was born in Tucson and educated at the University of Arizona, Indiana University, and Arizona State University. Her art has been exhibited since 1984 in Arizona and has been shown in New Mexico and California as well.

DRINKWATER'S SPECIAL SPAGHETTI SAUCE

1/2 C. olive oil (must be of a
    top grade)
3 onions sliced extremely thin
12 fresh med. size mushrooms
3 cloves garlic, mashed
2 lbs. meatballs
2 lbs. fresh Italian hot sausage
2 1/2 C. Bloody Mary mix
1 1/2 C. tomato puree
1 C. Italian tomato paste

1 lg. can Italian whole
    tomatoes
1 tsp. salt
1/2 tsp. pepper
1 tsp. sugar
4 jalapeño chile peppers
18 lg. king-size stuffed
    pimento olives

Put olive oil in large pot on medium heat. Sauté onions, garlic and mushrooms. Take those items out of the pot and put them in a dish. Make meatballs from your favorite recipe (must be made with **2 lbs. extremely lean ground chuck**). Cook meatballs and Italian sausage until approximately half done. Add the onions, garlic,

mushrooms, Bloody Mary mix, tomato puree, tomato paste, whole tomatoes, salt, pepper, and sugar. Put the 4 jalapeño peppers in the sauce whole. Simmer sauce for approximately 4 hours. Take the peppers out and discard them. Slice the olives in thin slices and put them in the sauce. Simmer for another 30 minutes.

Herb Drinkwater

Herb Drinkwater

Herb Drinkwater is the mayor of the city of Scottsdale.

FAMOUS TOMATO SAUCE

Brown:

4 Italian sausages - remove casing
1/4 lb. ground beef
1 medium onion, sliced thin
1/2 cup red wine

then add:

2 6 oz. cans tomato paste
2 1 lb.12 oz. cans crushed tomatoes with added puree
1 to 2 cloves crushed garlic
1/2 tsp. pepper
6 oz. water

Simmer covered for 8 hours. Uncover if it gets too watery.

While simmering add seasoning:

1/2 tsp. fennel seed	**1 tsp. basil**
2 tsp. parsley	**1 bay leaf**
1 tsp. sugar	**salt to taste**

Susan Gerard

Susan Gerard

Susan Gerard of Phoenix represents District 18 in the Arizona House of Representatives. The 41st Arizona Legislature (1993-1994) Directory lists her occupation as former retail manager and liaison to business community for the Arizona Department of Education. Committee assignments are: Banking & Insurance, Chair; Judiciary; Natural Resources; Agriculture & Rural Development. Susan provided us with a little trivia about her famous sauce: *"This is the famous Tomato Sauce reported about in The Arizona Republic and The Phoenix Gazette when the House Education Committee violated the Open Meeting Law at my home. I'm not on the Education Committee, so I didn't violate the law—I just enticed them!"*

WORLD'S GREATEST TACO SAUCE

1 sm. onion
1 28 oz. can of tomatoes
1 4 oz. can of green chiles, diced
2 tsp. Tabasco® sauce
1 tsp. salt

Dice the onion. Combine all of the ingredients in a blender. Blend just long enough to thoroughly mix everything. Store in the refrigerator.

John C. Keegan

John C. Keegan of Peoria represents District 19 in the Arizona House of Representatives. The 41st Arizona Legislature (1993-1994) Directory lists his occupation as professional engineer. Committee assignments are: Natural Resources; Agriculture & Rural Development, Chair; Appropriations; Judiciary.

"Many years ago, my wife, Mary, and I developed a recipe for taco sauce that we have enjoyed ever since. We hope that you and your readers will enjoy it, too. Mary and I wish you good luck in your book. Your goal of using the proceeds from the book to assist women in seeking independence from the welfare system is very commendable."

CHAMORRO FIESTA BARBECUE MARINADE

2 cloves chopped garlic
1 med. chopped onion
1/2 tsp. black pepper
juice from 2 lemons
1/2 C. vinegar
1 C. soy sauce
2 Tbsp. oil (if marinating chicken)

Mix ingredients together and marinate 3 to 4 pounds of meat (chicken, pork or rib-eye steak) for at least 2 hours.

Karen Barr

Karen Barr

Karen Barr is the publisher & editor of the magazine *Raising Arizona Kids*. "*Before I got married, I spent nearly 4 years as a journalist in Micronesia. As a reporter for the Pacific Daily News, I was based on the tiny island of Guam. I came to love Guamanian weekends. The native Chamorro villagers spent much of each weekend visiting each other's "fiesta"—which , I discovered, were held for virtually any kind of celebration, be it wedding, birthday, baptism or holiday. The tantalizing smell of barbecue wafted over the entire island—and any and all guests were welcome to drop by. To this day—and despite the many changes in my life that motherhood and owning a business have brought—chicken barbecued Chamorro-style is my favorite food. It takes me back to a time and place where life is simpler and where even small occasions are celebrated in a true spirit of sharing.*"

RUTH'S LOW CALORIE CRANBERRY RELISH

1 pkg. fresh or frozen cranberries
1/2 lg. orange plus rind
1 apple

Grind above ingredients using fine blade, or use food chopper. Add **1 cup crushed pineapple** in its own juice. Soften **1 tablespoon Knox® gelatin** in **1 cup low calorie cran-raspberry juice**. Heat to boiling to dissolve gelatin. Add **3/4 cup artificial sweetener (Sugar Twin Low Calorie Sugar Replacement®)**. Mix all together. Refrigerate. Will keep several weeks

George O. Pranspill

George O. Pranspill

George Pranspill is a leader of arts and cultural promotion in the Verde Valley area. Majoring in Engineering and Music gave George a broad range of talents to meet his career challenges and enjoy his retirement years. Residing for the past 6 years with his wife Ruth in Cottonwood, George spends his days doing volunteer work. He serves as first vice president of the Verde Valley Concert Association and vice president of Development for Marcus J. Lawrence Medical Center Foundation. For the past two years, he has served as chairman of a Joint Task Force of the above two organizations responsible for putting on two successful fund raisers—Vienna Choir Boys Concert in 1991 and two performances by the Eugene Ballet Company of the Nutcracker in 1992.

CHIMICHURRI
(Argentinean Spiced Parsley Sauce)

1/2 C. olive oil
1/4 C. red wine vinegar
1/2 C. onions, chopped fine
1 tsp. garlic, chopped fine
1/4 C. parsley, chopped
1 1/2 tsp. salt
1 tsp. oregano
1/4 tsp. cayenne
1 tsp. freshly ground pepper

In a bowl, combine the oil and vinegar and beat them with a fork. Stir in onions, garlic, parsley, oregano, cayenne, salt and pepper. Let stand at room temperature for 2-3 hours before serving. Use this sauce with grilled meats for basting. Excellent on steak, fish, pork, or chicken.

Theresa Matthews

Theresa Matthews

Theresa "Treats" Matthews is an artist who works wonders with her pottery by using bright, brilliant, vivid colors to enhance the beauty of her friendship pot, friendship lady, cactus pot, snakes, and chickens. Treats' main focus these days is fulfilling the heavy demand for orders from Scottsdale stores as well as shops in Sante Fe and California. Treats also loves working with metal and other materials in her creative designs.

SPICY SOUTHWESTERN SAUCE

1 16 oz. wine cooler
1 onion
1 green bell pepper
8 oz. of mushrooms
4 oz. of diced black olives
1 med. zucchini
8 oz. green chiles
2 oz. jalapeños
1 tsp. of garlic powder
2 8 oz. cans of tomato sauce
1 C. salsa (your favorite brand)

First put on a classical guitar tape or CD. Adjust volume to accommodate neighbors. Put on your apron, open the wine cooler, take a drink and begin! Dice onion, bell pepper, mushrooms, olives, zucchini, chiles and jalapeños very small. Heat a large frying pan to very hot. Put the garlic in the pan followed by the onions and peppers. Let these bounce around the pan for one minute. Turn the heat down to medium and add the rest of the vegetables. Slowly add the tomato sauce and the salsa. Now turn heat to low, cover and let simmer for 10 to 15 minutes. Meanwhile, you can finish your wine cooler. This sauce is perfect over chicken, pasta, or rice. Be sure and serve with bread as that will help control the heat being generated by the sauce.

Bruce Fischer

Bruce is a native Arizonan, a professional musician and a book publisher. He is still deciding between career choices of stand-up comedian or running for Entrepreneur of the Year. He is totally hooked on Mexican food and has been unable to leave the Valley for fear of withdrawal pains.

DUTCH OVEN YEAST ROLLS

4 pkgs. yeast in 4 1/2 C.
   lukewarm water
4 eggs
6 Tbsp. sugar (1 of it in yeast)
1 Tbsp. salt

1 C. powdered milk
2 sticks margarine or
   1 C. Wesson® Oil
4 lbs. flour (approx.)
8 to 9 pie or cake pans

Mix ingredients. Let stand about 20 minutes. Roll out dough to 1/2 to 3/4 inches thick. Cut with roll cutter (a vienna sausage can is ideal—punch a hole in top so roll will drop out.) Dip lightly in oil on both sides and fold over into parkerhouse shape. Put in pie pan or round cake pan almost touching and let raise. Bake in Dutch oven with coals top and bottom. Put 3 small rocks or bottle caps in bottom of oven and put baking pan on these to prevent burning on the bottom.

SELF FROSTING CINNAMON ROLLS

Proceed as above except: Add **6 tablespoons more sugar**, add **1/2 lb. raisins** to dough, if desired, during mixing. Roll dough 1/2 inch thick or less and about 6 to 8 inches wide. Sprinkle dough with **brown sugar** and **cinnamon** and roll into jelly roll shape for cutting. (Pinch edges to hold.) Cut sections 1 inch thick and place in prepared pan leaving room for expansion. Brush on top with melted margarine.

Preparing pans: Pour **3 tablespoons melted margarine** into baking pan. Sprinkle **brown sugar** to cover bottom. Add **chopped nuts**. Put rolls in pan on top of sugar and nuts. Let raise and bake. Turn out of pan immediately when done. Makes 100 rolls. Serves 40 people or 25 scouts.

Dilworth C. Brinton

Dilworth C. Brinton

Dilworth C. Brinton is a 1954 recipient of Mesa's Outstanding Citizen Award and was named Man of the Year. But his work did not stop then, it had only just begun. He is still very active in his community and he recently dedicated the Brinton Desert Botanical Gardens at the City of Mesa's Park of the Canals. He is often seen there tending to his cactus and strolling through the desert walk.

ZUCCHINI BREAD

3 beaten eggs
1 C. oil
2 C. sugar
2 C. grated zucchini
2 tsp. vanilla
3 C. flour

1/2 tsp. baking powder
1 tsp. salt
1 tsp. baking soda
2 tsp. cinnamon
3/4 C. nuts

Add oil, sugar, unpeeled zucchini and vanilla to eggs. Sift dry ingredients and add batter. Add nuts. Place in greased 7 x 4 x 2 pan at 350 degrees for 30 minutes.

Edward R. Beauvais

Ed Beauvais is the former chairman and chief executive officer of America West Airlines.

MY FAVORITE IRISH BREAD

2 C. flour
1 Tbsp. sugar
3 1/2 tsp. baking powder
1 tsp. salt (or less)

3 Tbsp. shortening
1 Tbsp. caraway seeds
3/4 C. raisins
1 C. milk

Sift and measure flour. Add sugar, baking powder and salt. Cut in shortening with 2 knives. Add raisins and caraway seeds, then milk. Mix well.

Spread dough in shallow pan. Bake in hot oven at 400 degrees about 30 minutes. Cut in thick slices.

Joann W. Kealiinohomoku

Joann W. Kealiinohomoku is program coordinator and acting executive director of Cross-Cultural Dance Resources, a non-profit organization she helped to establish in 1981. CCDR is dedicated to learning about all cultures through dance, with programs in research, consultation and performance, and is located in Flagstaff.

NAVAJO FRY BREAD

6 C. unbleached flour
3 Tbsp. baking powder
1 1/2 tsp. salt
1/4 C. powdered milk
vegetable oil

Mix all the dry ingredients together using your hands. Add warm water and knead until all dough is mixed and the dough is spongy. Cover and let sit for about an hour.

Heat about 2 inches of oil in a cast iron skillet. Have some flour on the side and take a small piece of dough a little larger than a golf ball and pat into a ball, then start to pull and flatten with your hands until you have stretched it into a tortilla shape. Lay carefully in the hot oil and brown on both sides. Drain it on a paper towel and sprinkle powdered sugar and honey or just plain salt or anything you like. Eat and enjoy.

Berta Benally

Berta Benally

The Jones Benally Family is a Native American Dance Troupe from Flagstaff. One of their main goals is to promote and share Native American cultures, predominantly the Navajo culture. They have travelled and performed throughout the world. The Bennally's also have a traditional Native American food booth and one of their most popular items is their Fry Bread.

DATE NUT BREAD

2 C. hot water
2 tsp. baking soda
2 C. dates, chopped
4 C. flour
1 1/2 C. sugar

1 tsp. salt
2 Tbsp. cooking oil
2 tsp. vanilla
2 eggs, beaten
1 C. nuts

Preheat oven to 350 degrees. Pour hot water and soda over dates. Let stand. Sift together flour, sugar, salt. Add cooking oil, vanilla, dates, beaten eggs. Mix well. Add nuts. Mix well again. Fill greased baking pans (small loaf) 2/3 full. Bake approximately 50 minutes. Remove from pans to cool. It freezes well and is delicious served warm with butter or cream cheese.

Pat & Lorraine Curry

Pat Curry is a graduate of Brigham Young University with a doctorate in Music Education. He taught ten years in high schools in Snowflake, Phoenix, and Tucson. In the '60s, he joined the Music Department at Northern Arizona Univeristy (then ASC-Flagstaff). He also served during that time as director of the Flagstaff Symphony Orchestra. He founded the Flagstaff Festival of the Arts. In 1973, he was awarded the Arizona Music Educator of the Year. He was honored as Flagstaff Citizen of the Year for 1986. He retired from NAU in 1987 and is a life member of Arizona Music Educators Association and Flagstaff Symphony Association. He also is a member of the board of the Flagstaff Festival of the Arts.

Lorraine Curry is a native of Arizona. She received her BA in Education (Music Major) at ASU and her MA in Education at NAU. She taught in elementary schools and joined the music staff in the Flagstaff Public Schools during the '60s. Later, she served as supervisor of music, supervisor of fine arts and then assistant superintendent for curriculum in Flagstaff. She received the 1975 Arizona Music Educator of the Year Award and was also honored as Flagstaff Citizen of the Year in 1985. She retired in 1986.

ARIZONA ORANGE ROLLS

1 cup scalded milk
1/2 cup shortening
1/3 cup sugar
1 tsp. salt
1 package yeast

1/4 cup warm water
2 eggs
1/4 cup orange juice
2 Tbsp. grated orange rind
5 cup flour

Mix together scalded milk, shortening, sugar, and salt in a large bowl. Cool to lukewarm. Dissolve yeast in warm water. Add beaten eggs, orange juice, and grated orange rind. Beat well. Add flour, mix to soft dough, cover and let stand 10 minutes. Knead dough 5 - 10 minutes on floured surface, when satin smooth and pliable place in greased bowl, turn over once to bring greased side to the top. Cover with a warm damp cloth and let rise in a warm place until double—about 2 hours. Punch down and let stand 15 minutes. Roll dough 10" x 16" x 1/2" thick. Cut strips 10" long by 3/4" wide, halve strips to 5", roll each strip lightly, knot and arrange on lightly greased baking sheet, tuck ends under. Cover, let rise until double. Bake at 400 degrees for 12 minutes. Remove from oven, place on rack. Brush on icing made by blending **2 TBSP orange juice, 1 tsp. grated orange rind, 1 cup confectioners sugar**. Use pastry brush for even coverage.

Mark Meyers

Mark Meyers

Mark Meyers is the airport director for Mesa-Falcon Field. Meyers is in charge of operation and maintenance of city-owned Falcon Field, and the development of airport property business.

(Author's note: A keen eye will detect a common sweetness among the Quayles (see page 91) and Meyers—although one is a tad sweeter than the other!)

JALAPEÑO CORN BREAD

"This makes good cowboys better!"

3 C. cornbread mix
1/2 C. oil
1 lg. grated onion
1 sm. can cream corn
1/2 C grated cheese
1/4 lb. crisp bacon (crumbled)
2 1/2 C. milk
3 eggs
2 Tbsp. sugar
1/2 C. chopped jalapeño peppers
1/4 C. chopped pimento
garlic powder to taste

Bake in greased skillet or pan for 30 minutes at 400 degrees. (batter will be thin).

Ben Johnson

Ben Johnson

Ben Johnson is a well-known movie and television actor. Most memorable is his Academy Award-winning role in *"The Last Picture Show"*. He also received the Golden Globe Award and the Peoples Choice Award for this movie. Johnson has been honored with numerous recognitions for his outstanding contributions to quality family entertainment as well as the Western Screen Heritage Award from the National Film Society. The Variety Club of Texas awarded him for his untiring efforts to enrich lives of disabled and disadvantaged children. One of his first films was *"The Outlaw"* released in 1941. His latest film in 1989 was, *"My Heroes Have Always Been Cowboys"*. Mr. Johnson resides in Arizona.

FIREMAN'S FAVORITE BANANA BREAD

Prepare before mixing: 3 bread pans greased well or use waxed paper on bottom

In very large bowl prepare:

1 1/2 C. canola oil
2 1/2 C. white sugar
5 eggs, well beaten
2 tsp. vanilla

In second bowl, prepare:

2 tsp. lemon juice
8 bananas, peeled and mashed

In third bowl prepare:

4 C. all-purpose flour
3 tsp. baking powder
3 tsp. baking soda
1 tsp. salt
2 C. walnuts, chopped
1 - 2 cups raisins, washed

Pour contents of second bowl in first bowl. Stir, then add contents of third bowl, slowly stirring until well mixed. Put in baking pans.

Bake in 325 degree oven for 1 hour. Cool. Wrap in waxed paper and foil. Freezes well.

Bruce S. McGregor Jr.

Bruce S. McGregor, Jr.

Bruce "Mitch" McGregor is an engineer and paramedic with the Mesa Fire Department. This recipe is a favorite of the "C" shift at station #4.

THE BEST ORANGE ROLLS WE EVER ATE

1 pkg. yeast	2 eggs, well beaten
1/4 C. warm water	1/4 C. orange juice
1 C. scalded milk, cooled	2 Tbsp. orange rind
1/2 C. shortening	5 C. flour
1 tsp. salt	

FROSTING

1 C. powdered sugar
1 can frozen orange juice concentrate, thawed

Soften yeast in warm water. Mix milk, shortening, salt and yeast mixture together. Add eggs, orange juice and orange rind. Beat well. Add flour, mixing to soft dough. Let stand 10 minutes.

Knead until pliable and place in greased bowl. Cover with damp cloth and let rise until mixture has doubled.

While dough is rising, prepare frosting. Add thawed orange juice concentrate to powdered sugar, a little at a time. Stir. Continue adding juice a little at a time until mixture has consistency of frosting. Set aside.

Shape into bowknots on greased cookie sheet. Bake in 400 degree oven until lightly browned.

Frost, serve warm, and enjoy!

Dan Quayle

Dan Quayle is the former vice president of the United States. The Quayle family lived in Paradise Valley, Arizona, during the 1950s and early '60s. Quayle is the grandchild of Eugene Pulliam, who owned *The Arizona Republic*, *Phoenix Gazette*, *Indianapolis Star* and smaller papers in Indiana. Dan's father, James Quayle, was the director of public relations for *The Republic* and *Gazette* in Arizona and eventually bought the *Huntington Herald Press*, which led the Quayle family back to Indiana in 1962.

CARROT, ZUCCHINI & APPLE MUFFINS

2 1/2 C. whole wheat flour
2 C. shredded carrots
1 1/4 C. sugar
1 C. shredded zucchini
1 Golden Delicious apple,
   cored and finely chopped
3/4 C. golden raisins
3/4 C. unsweetened shredded
   coconut, toasted
1/2 C. slivered almonds,
   toasted

1 Tbsp. cinnamon
1 tsp. nutmeg
2 tsp. baking soda
1 1/2 tsp. grated orange
   peel
1 tsp. vanilla extract
1/2 tsp. salt
3 lg. eggs
1 C. vegetable oil

Preheat oven to 375 degrees. Grease 1/2-cup muffin cups. Mix all ingredients except eggs and oil in large bowl. Beat eggs and oil in another bowl to blend. Stir flour mixture into eggs. Spoon batter to almost fill each cup. Bake until tester inserted in centers comes out clean, about 25 minutes.

Batter will keep a few days. Muffins can be frozen and reheated.

Harvey K. Smith

Harvey Smith has been the artistic director for the Phoenix Boys Choir since 1960. A native of Arizona, Dr. Smith received his education at Occidental College, University of Southern California and the University of Arizona, where he completed his doctorate. He has served as teacher of music in the Madison School, and in Phoenix Union High School districts, as choirmaster at various churches, and as a professor at Phoenix College. Much of the Phoenix Boys Choir's world-wide success is credited to Dr. Smith.

MANDEL BROT

3/4 C. margarine
1 C. sugar
3 eggs
2 tsp. vanilla
2 tsp. almond extract
2 tsp. orange juice

2 tsp. lemon juice
2 C. flour
1 tsp. baking powder
walnuts, raisins
cinnamon, sugar

Preheat oven to 350 degrees. Cream margarine and sugar. Add eggs, vanilla, almond extract, orange and lemon juices. Add flour and baking powder. Fold in nuts and raisins (use a lot of each). Form 2 loaves on greased cookie sheet. Sprinkle with mixture of cinnamon and sugar. Bake in 350 degree oven for 25 minutes.

Serve warm or freeze and slice and dip into coffee.

Marilyn Seymann

Marilyn R. Seymann

Marilyn Seymann is a nationally recognized business leader and is owner of a management and financial consulting firm. President Bush appointed her as a director and vice chair of the Federal Housing Finance Board. Marilyn is actively involved in chidren's issues, locally and nationally, and serves as the co-chairman of Arizona's Child Abuse Prevention Fund, vice president of the Crisis Nursery, the first woman director of the Boys & Girls Club of Metropolitan Phoenix and is a member of the board of directors of the Children's Welfare League of America. Marilyn and her husband have provided a foster home for dozens of children. She holds several honors including 1992 Citizen of the Year by the Arizona Chapter of the National Association of Social Workers. She is bilingual in English and Spanish and has been published in both languages.

CORN MUFFINS a la RONSTADT

1 C. whole wheat flour
1 C. yellow corn meal,
    whole meal
4 tsp. baking powder
1/2 tsp. salt (optional)

1/4 C. sugar
2 eggs, lightly beaten
1 C. skim milk
3 Tbsp. butter, melted
1 C. creamed style corn

Combine first 5 ingredients in large bowl. In medium bowl, combine eggs, milk, butter and corn. Add this to dry ingredients, stirring until dry ingredients are moistened. Spoon batter into 12 greased muffin cups. Bake in 425 degree preheated oven for 20-25 minutes or until tops are golden.

Linda Ronstadt

Linda Ronstadt

Linda Ronstadt is an internationally known singer from Tucson, Arizona. She has recorded numerous albums including her most recent *Mas Canciones* in 1991 and *Frenesi* in 1992. She received Grammy awards in 1975, 1976, 1987, 1988 (with Emmylou Harris & Dolly Parton), 1989 & 1990 (with Aaron Neville), and 1992. The American Music Award was given to her in 1978. In 1989 she received an Emmy Award for *Canciones De Mi Padre*. She received the Academy of Country Music award in 1987 and 1988. Linda Marie Ronstadt often performs Spanish songs and she recently sang at the International Mariachi Conference in Tucson. A television announcement was made during her performance soliciting bone marrow donations from Hispanics to help in the transplants of ethnic groups who are unable to provide sibling donors.

WHEAT BREAD RECIPE

2 (heaping) Tbsp. dry yeast
1/2 C. lukewarm water

Dissolve yeast in water until it is active. If not active in 20 minutes, add teaspoon of sugar. Pour into large bowl and add:

6 C. water
2 Tbsp. salt
1/2 C. honey or sugar
1/4 C. oil
1 egg
8 to 10 C. flour (part wheat and part white)

Add more flour if needed to make a good dough. Knead until dough is smooth and pliable (about 10 minutes). Let rise once and place in pans (cans*). Let rise again to double in size and bake in 350 degree oven for 40 minutes.

*I bake my bread in large round juice cans. Most ovens will hold 7 to 12 cans at one time. Be sure sides of cans do not touch.

Junith H. Roberts

Junith H. Roberts

Junith Roberts of Arizona is the president of the Daughters of Utah Pioneers.

WHOLE WHEAT BREAD

1 1/2 Tbsp. dry yeast	1/2 to 1 C. sesame seeds
1 C. warm water	1 C. sunflower seeds
7 1/4 C. water	1 C. cornmeal
1 or 2 Tbsp. salt	1 C. oatmeal
3/4 C. vegetable oil	12 C. whole wheat flour
3/4 C. honey	3 C. unbleached white flour

Soak yeast in warm water (in large bowl) until dissolved. Add remaining water. Stir in salt, oil and honey, using heavy wooden spoon. Add next 4 ingredients, stirring after each one. Add all flour and stir until well mixed. It will be quite stiff and sticky! Cover and let sit for 4 to 5 hours.

When time is up, oil 6 glass loaf pans. Dump dough onto well-floured surface and knead as long as you can. Ten minutes is great! Divide dough into 6 equal portions. Knead each portion, shape into loaf and put into pan. Cover and let rise.

Set oven at 350 degrees (may be less depending on oven). When bread rises to top of pans, put into oven and bake 45 to 50 minutes. When done, take pans out of oven and let sit for 2 to 3 minutes. Loosen sides with knife and dump bread out onto racks. Let cool completely to slice neatly. Cut immediately for a wonderful, warm slice of bread!

Larry Reid

Larry Reid

Larry Reid is managing director of Flagstaff Festival of the Arts. (Author's note: He is also one of the most dedicated and loyal fans of over 30 people contributing recipes in this cookbook. I sent a letter to Larry soliciting his recipe for this cookbook and not only did I receive his recipe, I was sent a healthy list of people, people that have made a difference, that he wanted to include in the cookbook as well. I was delighted and overwhelmed at his thoughtfulness. I am glad I have the opportunity to thank him for his gracious contribution. I hope his friends know who recommended them to me! If you didn't before, now you know!)

GET RID OF THOSE BROWN BANANAS BREAD

**1 C. mashed bananas or those brown bananas
that no one wants to eat!**
1/3 C. shortening
1/2 C. sugar
2 eggs
1 3/4 C. flour
2 tsp. baking powder
1/4 tsp. baking soda
1 C. walnuts

Mix and beat shortening, sugar, eggs and bananas. Mix in all other ingredients and add walnuts. Pour into 9 x 5 greased loaf pan. Bake in 350 degree oven for 1 hour. Remove from pan after 10 minutes and cook on rack.

Variations: Add chopped dates, raisins, or grated orange peel.

James Threadgill

James Threadgill

Jim Threadgill is the mayor of Cave Creek, a community settled in 1870, incorporated in 1986.

DILL BREAD

(by Joyce Holmes)

1 Tbsp. minced instant onion	1 tsp. salt
1 Tbsp. soft butter	1/4 tsp. soda
2 tsp. dill seed	1 egg

Mix all together. Add **1 cup creamed cottage cheese**, heated warm. Add **1 package yeast** dissolved in **1/4 cup warm water**. Add **2 Tbsp. sugar** and **2 1/2 cups flour**. Mix well, knead.

Place in greased bowl. Let rise until double (1 1/4 hours). Mash down. Let rise 40 minutes. Bake in 350 degree oven for 40 to 50 minutes. Brush with **salt** and **butter**.

Gregg Holmes

Gregg Holmes is the vice president/general manager of Dimension Cable in Phoenix. Gregg is very active in the community, serving as vice-chairman of the board of the Phoenix Chamber of Commerce, a member of the Excellence in Education Commission, a board member of the Phoenix Memorial Hospital Foundation, a board member of the Phoenix Symphony, a trustee of the Arizona State University Foundation at the Walter Cronkite School of Journalism and a board member of the Peoria Economic Development Group. He comments that community involvement offers tremendous personal reward and serves as an opportunity to work on issues that are critical to the future and well-being of the Valley. His primary concerns are the future and strength of our educational system, the image and reputation of the Valley, and the strength and vitality of the Valley's economy. *"As a kid growing up in West Texas, my mother used to make these recipes on special occasions. To this day, when I eat them, I think of the great times we had as a family. Especially on holidays when everyone would gather at our house, these recipes were the talk of the night. There's nothing better than biting into a piece of brisket you can cut with a fork and fresh baked bread just out of the oven covered with butter."*

FIRST TUESDAY IN NOVEMBER BEER BREAD

This recipe is so simple and quick that it can be prepared even on election day!

one room-temperature bottle of beer (12 oz.)
one very cold bottle of beer (12 oz.)
3 C. of self-rising flour
3 Tbsp. sugar

Mix the warm beer, the flour and the sugar with a spoon until flour is moist. Place mixture in a buttered loaf pan and bake for 45 minutes at 350 degrees.

(Drink the cold bottle of beer while waiting!)

Serve bread warm, immediately after baking.

Marilyn Evans

Marilyn Evans

Marilyn Evans is the president and chief executive officer for Kids Voting USA, which is headquartered in Tempe. The aim of the program is to instill the voting habit in kids so that when they become adults, going to the polls on election day will be second nature. Along the way, it is hoped that kids going to the polls will also encourage their parents to do so, too.

LUNCH TIME SNACK

olive oil
1 white onion, sliced
    1/4" thick or less
2 cloves of garlic, diced

1/4 lb. tofu, sliced 1/4" thick
1/4 red pepper, diced
2 brown eggs
Greek olives

Heat iron skillet covered with thin layer of olive oil. Place sliced onions flat in skillet. Add diced garlic. Add sliced tofu making sure all contents touch skillet surface. When contents begin to brown, turn ingredients over and reduce to medium heat. Add diced red peppers. Crack 2 brown eggs on over cooking mixture. Put lid on pan. Wait for three minutes. Serve immediately—top with Greek olives or picante sauce.

John Waddell

John Waddell is an internationally renowned sculptor who resides in Cornville. Among other honors, he was recently inducted into the new Sedona Artist Hall of Fame.

DEPRESSION POT PIE
(Potatoes, Wieners & Cheese)

mashed potatoes (instant or fresh) to fill
    dish 1 to 1 1/2" deep
hot dogs sliced to 3/4" length (beef franks) inserted
    randomly in potatoes
grated cheese to cover
salsa for extra zip

Bake at 350 degrees until cooked and cheese melts. Serve and enjoy.

Robert V. Chapman

Robert V. Chapman is the executive Presbyter, Presbytery of Grand Canyon, Presbyterian Church (U.S.A.)

EPINARD A LA CREPE DE FROMAGE CHAUDE

(Warm Cheese Crepe on Spinach with Hearts of Palm)

8 thin slices Brie or blue
   cheese, at room temperature
8 very thin crepes
fresh spinach leaves
1 carrot, cut into julienne
8 canned hearts of palm, cut into 2-inch pieces

4 cherry tomatoes
12 black olives
vinaigrette dressing
1/4 cup minced walnuts

Lay a slice of cheese on each crepe and fold over ends and sides to form rectangular-shaped package. Heat in microwave oven just until cheese melts and crepes are hot, about 45 seconds.

Arrange spinach in rosette pattern on individual small plates and top with 2 of the warm crepes and cheese. Garnish with carrot, hearts of palm, cherry tomatoes and black olives. Drizzle vinaigrette over crepes and vegetables, then sprinkle with walnuts. Yield: 4 servings

Cameron Harper

Cameron Harper is news anchor for KTVK-TV, Channel 3 News, in Phoenix.

GREEN CHILE CHICKEN CASSEROLE

1 dozen corn tortillas
1/2 pt. chopped green chile (2-4 oz. cans)
1/2 lb. grated sharp cheese (or more; I usually use
    Jack or longhorn)
1 lg. onion, chopped
1 can cream of chicken soup (or cream of mushroom soup)
1 lg. can evaporated milk (12 oz.)
1 can of chicken (12 1/2 oz.)
Add sliced black olives to mixture or as garnish (if desired)

Tear tortillas in small pieces (about 2" to 3" pieces) into large bowl. Add remainder of ingredients and mix thoroughly. Butter (margarine) another large casserole for baking.

Bake at 325 degrees for about an hour. This can be made and frozen ahead. Cook it a little and cool before freezing, then finish cooking when needed for use.

This whole recipe can be vegetarian by substituting mushroom soup for chicken soup, and by eliminating the chicken. I have made it without chicken and it is just as wonderful; in fact, we prefer it that way.

Brenda A. Cole
M. David Meeker

Brenda A. Cole and M. David Meeker

Brenda Cole is a graduate of the New England Conservatory of Music. Her accompanying and performing experience includes Cochise College and Buena High School in Sierra Vista, as well as other works in Massachusetts. She has made appearances on radio, television, theatre, chorus, and piano (singing and accompanying).

M. David Meeker obtained his music degrees from the University of Arizona. He is a professor of Vocal Music, Drama and Art at Cochise College, Sierra Vista and also an artist with one-man shows in southern Arizona. He is a member of the Governor's Task Force on the Arts and on the grants panel of the Arizona Commission on the Arts.

GREEN CHILE ENCHILADA CASSEROLE

1 lb. ground beef	1 pkg. 6" flour tortillas cut
1 clove garlic	or torn into strips
1 med. onion, chopped	1- 4oz. can chopped green chiles
1 1/2 tsp. comino	1 lb. grated Jack cheese
1 1/2 tsp. oregano	1-12 oz. bottle Ortega®
salt and pepper to taste	Green Chile Salsa
1-15 oz. can tomato sauce	1 sm. can evaporated milk

Brown meat with garlic, onion, and spices. Drain excess fat. Stir in tomato sauce and set aside.

Prepare a greased baking dish (5 qt. size). Layer as follows: tortillas, beef, chiles, cheese, Ortega salsa. Repeat layers until ingredients are used and last layer is salsa. Add evaporated milk around the edges only. Cover and cook for approximately 30 minutes on high in the microwave or at 350 degrees in the oven. Milk will keep tortillas soft.

Yield: Serves 8 to 10 people.

Judy Borgeson

Judy Borgeson

Judy Borgeson is the director and founder of Shoebox Ministry in Scottsdale - a ministry for the collection and distribution of toiletry items to the homeless. She was awarded one of the 1992 "12 Who Care Hon Kachina Awards." The Luke's Men of St. Luke's Medical and Behavioral Health Centers and KPNX-Channel 12 honor twelve outstanding volunteers for their contributions to humanity. The Hon Kachina, according to legend, represents great healing powers. Because each of these recipients have been so giving of themselves and assisted in the healing of others, they have been awarded the Hon Kachina symbolizing excellence in volunteer service.

PORK CHOPS & SCALLOPED POTATOES

4 to 5 medium raw
   potatoes, sliced
1 raw onion, sliced
salt and pepper to taste
1 can cream of
   mushroom soup

3/4 can milk
4 to 5 pork chops
2 eggs beaten
1 dish cracker crumbs
   (saltine)
3 Tbsp. oil

In greased casserole dish, put layers of potatoes, onion, and seasonings. Mix soup and milk and pour into casserole. Put in 350 degree oven for 45 minutes. Fifteen minutes before potatoes are done, dip chops in eggs, then cracker crumbs. Brown in frying pan with oil. Place browned chops on top of potatoes and onion. Cover and bake 350 degrees in oven for 45 minutes more. Total cooking time 1 1/2 hours.

Joe Bugel

Joe Bugel is in his fourth season as the head coach for the Phoenix Cardinals. As former Washington Redskins assistant coach for nine years, he holds two Super Bowl rings (1983 and 1988 Super Bowl wins) from three Super Bowl appearances. Coach Bugel was born in Pittsburgh, Pennsylvania where he worked in the steel mills after graduating from high school. After a couple of weeks, he knew that was not the life for him, so he pursued a sports career. After 15 years of assistant coaching, he posted a 144-82 composite record (.637), in a span that included 13 winning seasons, 8 playoff appearances (21 games), 6 conference championship games, and 3 Super Bowls.

NO-WORK CHICKEN

4 - 6 chicken breasts   **1 Tbsp. curry powder**
1/2 cup honey   **2 Tbsp. soy sauce**
1/2 cup Dijon style wet mustard

Place chicken snuggly, skin side down, in flat baking dish in one layer. Make marinade by mixing together the honey, mustard, curry powder and soy sauce. Pour over chicken and refrigerate 2 - 6 hours, or overnight for curry flavor. When ready, turn chicken, cover dish with foil, and bake 350 degrees for 1 hour. Remove foil and baste well and continue baking uncovered for 15 minutes. When serving, spoon sauce over chicken.

Ryan Matthews

Ryan Matthews

Ryan Matthews is an 11-year-old (soon to be twelve) who recently was honored by being asked to join the Metropolitan Youth Symphony. Ryan started learning to read music and play the bass in the fourth grade at an elementary school in the Mesa Unified School District. MYS, organized in 1982 to provide a challenging program of excellence in orchestral music for young musicians, performs at various locations throughout the valley including festivals, high schools, Chandler Center for the Arts and Arizona State University Recital Hall. Though its 290 members are mostly from the east valley, their training program is open to all Arizona musicians through the ninth grade. (Author's note: I recently heard Ryan play bass in Division IV for MYS at the Chandler Center for the Arts and was delighted with the accomplishments of these young performers.)

POULET d'ARTICHOKE

2 pkgs. of frozen artichoke hearts
olive oil
2 garlic cloves
2 2/3 C. cubed cooked chicken
2 cans cream of chicken soup
1 C. mayonnaise
1 tsp. lemon juice
1/2 tsp. curry powder
1 1/4 C. shredded sharp cheddar cheese
1 C. bread cubes
2 Tbsp. melted butter

Cook artichokes according to package directions adding a little olive oil and 2 garlic cloves.

Drain cooked artichokes and arrange in a greased 9 x 12 baking dish. Spread chicken on top of the artichokes.

Combine and mix well the soup, mayonnaise, lemon juice and curry powder. Pour over the chicken. Sprinkle with grated cheese.

Toss bread cubes in melted butter to coat. Scatter on top of cheese. Bake 350 degrees for 25 minutes.

Yield: Serves 8 (can be made ahead and cooked later).

Dean C. Borgman

Dean C. Borgman is the president of McDonnell Douglas Helicopter Company in Mesa.

SPARERIBS AND SAUERKRAUT

Using large pot or pressure cooker, brown desired quantity of **pork spareribs** (large rib best) in hot **cooking oil** with **salt, black pepper**, and **caraway seed**. Remove browned ribs from pot and pour out oil and grease. Place ribs back in pot and add water to cover ribs and add more caraway seed. Cover and boil slowly, approximately 2 hours (pressure cooker—approximately 30 minutes) until meat is very tender. Add desired quantity of **sauerkraut** sprinkled with caraway seed* and simmer for approximately 15 minutes (pressure cooker - bring to a boil, turn off, and let pressure drop gradually).

*Add **sliced potatoes** or **dumplings** if desired and extend the cooking time to 30 minutes (5 minutes for pressure cooker).

Dave Carson

Dave Carson

Dave Carson of Prescott formerly represented District 1 in the Arizona House of Representatives. The 40th Arizona Legislature (1991-1992) Directory lists his occupation as general contractor/businessman. Committee assignments were: Licensing, Professions and Tourism, Chairman; Financial Institutions and Insurance; Environment; Rules; Ways and Means.

HERRING COPENHAGEN

For marinated herring:

1 dozen herring fillets in brine
1 whole herring in brine water
1 C. distilled white vinegar
1/2 C. finely granulated sugar
1/4 tsp. ground allspice

1/2 tsp. ground white pepper
4 bay leaves
1/2 C. coarsely chopped
   Bermuda onion

Place filets and whole herring in large enamel or earthenware bowl. Add cold water to cover. Soak herring overnight to remove excess salt, changing water several times. Drain herring. Cut each fillet crosswise into 1-inch pieces. Place pieces in enamel or earthenware bowl. Prepare whole herring in similar manner. Cut crosswise into 1-inch pieces. Place in separate bowl. Place remaining ingredients in saucepan. Bring to boil. Simmer 1 minute. Remove from heat. Cool to room temperature. Pour most of the marinade over fillets. Pour remainder over whole herring pieces. Cover bowls. Let herring marinate in refrigerator 6 hours or longer. Drain, reserve marinade. Serve herring plain, using pieces cut from whole herring for garnish or use in many ways for main dish or salad offerings. Yield: Serves 25.

Walter Cronkite

Walter Cronkite served as CBS News correspondent for 31 years, including nearly 19 years as anchor and managing editor, and has been a special correspondent for CBS since stepping down from his anchor position in 1981.

Mr. Cronkite has received numerous awards for his achieve-

(continued on next page)

(Walter Cronkite—continued from previous page)

ments in journalism—among them are a Presidential Medal of Freedom, two Peabody Awards, the National Association of Broadcasters' Distinguished Service Award and several Emmys.   Mr. Cronkite is a frequent visitor to Arizona, where he maintains an active interest in the Walter Cronkite School of Journalism and Telecommunications at Arizona State University.

ROAST PORK & SAUERKRAUT

2 lbs. pork roast
flour
1 med. finely chopped onion
4 buds garlic, chopped fine
1 tsp. allspice
1 can sauerkraut, well rinsed

Dredge pork roast in flour and brown in dutch oven. Add other ingredients. Cook 2 hours on top of stove or in oven.

Remove meat. Thicken gravy. Serve gravy and sauerkraut over mashed potatoes.

Bob Denny

Bob Denny

Bob Denny of Litchfield Park is a former state senator representing District 15. The 40th Arizona Legislature (1991-1992) Directory lists his occupation as retired colonel, United States Air Force. Committee assignments were: Finance; Government; Judiciary.

PASTA E FAGIOLI
(Pasta & Beans)

2 oz. either cut macs or elbow macaroni (uncooked)
3 C. spaghetti sauce
1 C. sliced celery
1 can navy beans
1/4 C. Parmesan or Romano grated cheese

Cook pasta as package directs; drain water. Heat spaghetti sauce and celery over medium heat until it starts to boil, stirring occasionally. Reduce heat and simmer five to seven minutes or until celery is crisp tender. Drain juice from can of beans and stir beans in sauce. Cook until beans are heated through and toss sauce with beans on the pasta. Top with cheese.

Note: Heat the sauce and beans before you cook the pasta. This way when you have the pasta cooked, the sauce and beans are hot and so is the pasta. Buon appetito!

Tom Damiano

Tom Damiano is the former mayor of the city of Apache Junction.

FLANK STEAK

1 1/2 - 2 pounds flank steak tenderized

STUFFING

3 strips bacon	**1 tsp. salt**
2 slices bread	**1/2 tsp. sage**
1 C. apple slices	**1/4 tsp. pepper**
1/4 C. diced onion	**1/4 tsp. thyme**

Lay flank steak on board. Spread stuffing in order given; roll up and secure with skewers or tooth picks and string. Put steak in ovenware, pour **1 1/2 cups apple juice** over all. Cover tightly and bake at 350 degrees for 1 1/2 hours. Remove cover last ten minutes to brown steak. Turn oven off and put steak on a platter. Recover with foil and put back in oven to keep warm while making sauce.

SAUCE

1/2 C. sour cream	**3/4 tsp. Worcestershire sauce**
3/4 C. pan dripping	**1 1/2 Tbsp. cornstarch**
1/4 tsp. onion salt	**1 1/2 Tbsp. water**

Pour a full cup of pan drippings, let settle and take off excess fat to 3/4 cup. Mix cornstarch and water and blend all ingredients well with wire whisk in saucepan and heat just to boiling point stirring constantly. Serve immediately.

Bill Denney

Bill Denney

Bill Denney is news anchor and sports director for KPNX-TV, Channel 12 News, in Phoenix.

EASY CHICKEN CURRY

4 Tbsp. butter
1/2 C. chopped onion
2 tsp. curry powder
2 Tbsp. flour
1 tsp. ginger
1 tsp. salt
1 tsp. sugar
1 C. milk
1 C. chicken broth (or bouillon)
2 C. cooked chicken, cut in small pieces
1 Tbsp. lemon juice

Melt butter in large skillet. Add onion and curry powder. Sauté until onion is clear. Add flour, ginger, salt and sugar. Stir until mixture is bubbly. Add milk and broth. Cook on low heat, stirring occasionally, until mixture is thickened slightly. Add chicken and lemon juice. Heat through. Serve over rice.

Serve condiments to be sprinkled over curry as desired: Chutney, bacon bits, peanuts, raisins, coconut, crushed pineapple, cucumber, etc.

Fred J. Dees

Fred J. Dees is the chief of police for the town of Gilbert.

VEAL SCALLOPINI

3 lbs. veal round, thinly sliced
1/4 C. flour
salt and pepper
4 Tbsp. olive oil
3 med. onions, finely chopped
2 sprigs parsley
1 4-oz. can mushrooms
1/2 C. white Sauterne wine

Cut veal into 2" slices, shake in flour and season with salt and pepper. Heat oil in a large skillet and brown veal, add onions and parsley and stir until onions are brown. Add mushrooms in liquid, adding water if necessary. Cover tightly and cook over low heat for 1 hour. If mixture is not brown enough, add a little Kitchen Bouquet®. Add wine half an hour before serving to avoid evaporation.

Yield: Serves 6.

Dennis De Concini

Dennis DeConcini

Dennis DeConcini represents Arizona in the United States Senate. A graduate of the University of Arizona, he was elected to the United States Senate in 1976. DeConcini, in his 16th year as a senator, is the first Arizonan to chair a senate committee since Barry Goldwater. He chairs the Senate Intelligence Committee and the Commission on Security and Cooperation in Europe (Helsinki Commission). This family recipe is the senator's favorite.

MAYOR FORGIA'S ROLLED TACOS

cooking oil
1 dozen corn tortillas
1 lb. cooked and shredded roast beef
1 lb. grated cheese
1 med. chopped onion
1 sm. can chopped olives
toothpicks
chile salsa

Heat cooking oil in a skillet large enough to fry three rolled tacos at a time. Dip the corn tortillas in the hot oil just long enough to soften. Lay hot tortilla flat on several layers of newspaper that have been covered with wax paper. Place a row of shredded beef off center on the tortilla, pressing the beef down slightly. Repeat this process with the cheese, onions and olives. After placing all ingredients on the tortilla, roll the tortilla up, using a toothpick to keep it from unrolling. Press in gently on each end as you finish rolling each taco. Repeat until all are rolled. Add enough oil to skillet to fry tacos, heating oil to 375 - 400 degrees. Fry tacos to desired crispness, drain and serve as soon as they are cool enough to handle. Serve with mild or hot chile salsa. Recipe ingredients can be multiplied for the desired number of tacos.

Yield: Makes one dozen.

Ken C. Forgia

Ken C. Forgia

Ken C. Forgia is the mayor of the city of Peoria.

GREEN CHILE CHICKEN CHEESE ENCHILADA

Layer one:

1 pkg. corn tortillas (soften by dipping in and out of boiling water in a skillet)

Layer two-sauce:

2 cans of cream of chicken soup
1 can of chopped green chile
1 1/3 C. milk
1 or 2 cans white chicken or turkey
1 med. onion, chopped

Layer three:

1 lb. colby cheese, shredded

Mix sauce ingredients in a pan on the stove and cook until hot. In a large glass baking dish, layer tortillas, sauce and then cheese. Begin same process making another layer of tortillas, sauce and ending up with cheese. Bake at 325 degrees for approximately 40 minutes or until cheese is bubbly.

Delicious with hot sauce, lettuce and black olives served on the side.

Tom Freestone

Tom Freestone

Tom Freestone of Mesa is a former member of the Maricopa County Board of Supervisors. After a 14-year tenure on the board, he retired in 1992, after serving longer than any other supervisor in Maricopa County history. He was Mesa Man of the Year in 1990.

STACKED ENCHILADAS

2 Tbsp. flour
2 Tbsp. oil
4 C. water
16 oz. can tomato puree
1 sm. can tomato paste
1 Tbsp. garlic powder
3 Tbsp. hot chili powder
1/2 Tbsp. cumin
1 Tbsp. oregano

1/2 tsp. salt
1/2 tsp. black pepper
1 head lettuce
1 onion
1 lb. sharp cheddar cheese
1 C. corn oil for frying pan
1 dozen fresh corn tortillas
8 eggs (fried - optional)

Take sauce pan and mix flour and oil with no heat until blended well. Add water, the tomato puree and tomato paste. Turn heat to high until boiling. Reduce to simmer and add garlic powder, chili powder, cumin, oregano, salt, and pepper. Stir well. Simmer for 4 hours, covered (for faster meals - 2 hours). Stir every 1/2 hour.

After the sauce has thickened (take lid off last 45 minutes of cooking if you need to thicken up more) turn off heat. Chop in separate bowl the lettuce, onions, and cheese. Take large frying pan and add 1 cup corn oil. Heat oil on medium to high heat until top heat and dip tortillas one at a time for about 20 seconds on each side. Take out and drop into sauce. Cover tortilla completely with sauce. Put tortilla on large single plate. Sprinkle cheese on top followed by some onion and lettuce. Repeat process with a new tortilla. Make sure you stack these on a layer at a time. A 4-stack is if you are really hungry or if you sky surf at 13,000 feet like me. Happy Eating, and oh, by the way, fry two eggs per person and put on top for an even better dish! Yield: Serves 4.

Russell Calkins

Russell Calkins is president of Currencies & Metals Investments, specializing in precious metals, rare coins and numismatics. But more interestingly, he jumps from airplanes at 13,000 feet with a 55-inch aluminum board strapped to his feet. The Scottsdale businessman is a "skysurfer" who performs flips and somersaults while hurtling through the sky. He is becoming nationally known. Good Luck, Russell. We'll be watching for you in the sky.

BETTER THAN ANN LANDERS MEAT LOAF

1 1/2 lbs. lean ground beef
1 egg
1 pkg. Lipton® Onion Soup mix
1 med. onion, chopped
1 1/4 C. V-8® juice
3/4 C. quick oatmeal

Mix all ingredients adding oatmeal last.

TOPPING
2/3 C. catsup
2 - 3 Tbsp. brown sugar
1 - 2 tsp. prepared mustard
1 Tbsp. Worcestershire sauce

Mix ingredients and put in loaf pan. Mix topping and pour over loaf. Bake at 325 degrees for 1 1/2 hours.

Albert "Lefty" Freestone

Albert "Lefty" Freestone

Albert Freestone was recently honored as a 1992 Inductee into the Mesa City Sports Hall of Fame. "Lefty" was an All State football player and pitcher at Mesa High School in 1932. A permanent Hall of Fame display is being developed by the Mesa Historical Society and will be housed at the Crismon Heritage Museum in Mesa.

LINGUINE WITH WHITE CLAM SAUCE

2 Tbsp. chopped onions
2 tsp. chopped garlic
1/2 C. olive oil
2 Tbsp. dried parsley
1/2 C. white wine
2 cans (5 ounces) whole baby clams
linquine
1 Tbsp. butter or margarine
2 Tbsp. grated Parmesan cheese

Sauté onions and garlic in olive oil. When the onion is translucent and the garlic lightly colored, add parsley. Stir. Remove from heat.

Measure out wine in mixing cup. Drain juice from the clams and add to the wine. Pour into the olive oil mixture. If the mixture is too hot, the wine will sizzle and evaporate. Return to heat and simmer, uncovered, for 10 minutes. Cook and drain linguine. Add clams, butter and Parmesan cheese to sauce. Stir. Serve over linguine.

John A. Greene

John Greene

John Greene of Phoenix is an Arizona state senator representing District 24. The 41st Arizona Legislature (1993-1994) Directory lists his occupation as attorney. Committee assignments are: Senate President; Rules.

ENCHILADAS

4 or 5 buds garlic
3 Tbsp. cooking oil
3 Tbsp. (approx.) flour
2 cans El Pato® tomato sauce
   with chiles frescas

warm water (2 cans)
2 half-rounds longhorn
   cheddar cheese
chopped onions (optional)
1 dozen corn tortillas

Chop the garlic fine and sauté in cooking oil (I use olive oil). When slightly brown, remove pot from fire and mix in flour to form a thick roux. Add tomato/chili sauce slowly, stirring into roux. Then add two cans warm water and stir in. This is the enchilada sauce. Add more water if needed to thin it; if it seems too thin, just let it simmer on low heat—it will thicken quickly.

While sauce simmers, heat small frying pan half-filled with oil, and grate cheese. Chop onions coarsely, if you want them. When a piece of tortilla dropped into the oil fries up crisp, the oil is hot enough.

Using tongs, dip a tortilla into hot oil briefly—no more than four or five seconds. Remove and let excess oil drip off, then dip the tortilla into enchilada sauce so that most of tortilla is coated with sauce. Lay tortilla on dinner plate, sprinkle thick line of grated cheese across middle. If you wish to add onions, sprinkle them thinly over the cheese. Roll up tortilla and place in baking dish. When all enchiladas are made, pour remaining sauce over them and garnish with a little grated cheese. Bake at 350 degrees for ten minutes or until cheese if visibly melted. Serve with cold beer or soft drinks.

Diana Gabaldon

Diana Gabaldon

Diana Gabaldon of Scottsdale is the local author of the 1991 national best seller *Outlander* and the 1992 sequel *Dragonfly in Amber*. She is finishing up her third novel. She has been reading technical books for *Recording for the Blind* for the last 11 years. A tidbit from Diana: "*My father, Tony Gabaldon, insists that it's cheating to use tomato sauce with the chile already in it, but I do anyway*".

SALMON a la HOON

6 pcs. salmon fillet
1 oz. sesame oil
1 1/2 C. teriyaki sauce
6 oz. soba noodles*, cooked and chilled
8 oz. baby green beans, blanched and refreshed
1 1/2 C. ginger butter sauce*
1 red bell pepper, 1/8" small dice
1/2 C. Amazu Shoga (pickled ginger)*
1 packet enoki mushrooms

Sear salmon fillet in a little sesame oil, searing hard on both sides. Deglaze with teriyaki sauce, cook until salmon is medium-rare and nicely glazed. Heat cooked soba noodles in a little teriyaki sauce. Sauté blanched baby green beans in a little ginger butter sauce. Present salmon on a bed of soba noodles surrounded with ginger butter sauce, a bouquet of baby green beans, and sprinkled with diced red peppers. Garnish with pickled ginger with enoki mushrooms standing up.

*Available in Oriental food stores.

Ron Hoon

Ron Hoon is news anchor for KPNX-TV, Channel 12 News, in Phoenix. Franklin Biggs, executive chef at The Buttes' Top of the Rock, and Hoon created this delightful dish for a 1993 Waste Not Celebrity Chef Challenge. Fifty percent of the entrees' proceeds benefit Waste Not, a non-profit Valley organization dedicated to combating hunger. Bobbi Jo Haynes, manager of Top of the Rock, was very helpful in getting this recipe.

CHICKEN PARMESAN

3 whole chicken breast, cut
   in half, boned, & skinned
1/3 C. all purpose flour
1/2 tsp. salt
1/8 tsp. white pepper
1/8 tsp. ground nutmeg
1/8 tsp. marjoram leaves
1 egg beaten with 1 Tbsp. water

1/3 C. fine dry bread crumbs
1/4 C. freshly grated
   Parmesan cheese
1/4 C. butter or margarine
2 Tbsp. olive oil
2 C. spaghetti sauce
1 C. mozzarella cheese
2 Tbsp. Parmesan cheese

Place chicken breast, one at a time, between pieces of wax paper or plastic wrap and pound with flat side of mallet until 1/4 inches thick. Mix flour, salt, pepper, nutmeg, and marjoram in shallow dish. Have egg mixture ready in second shallow dish. Mix crumbs an 1/4 cup Parmesan cheese in a third. Coat chicken breasts lightly with flour mixture, then with egg, and finally with crumb mixture.

In a wide frying pan over medium-high heat, place butter and oil. When butter is melted, add chicken breasts, without crowding, and cook, turning over once, until golden brown on each side (about 2 to 3 minutes per side). Spoon 1/4 cup Spaghetti Sauce in a 9 x 13 inch pan. Put chicken breasts on sauce and cover with remaining sauce. Sprinkle 1 cup mozzarella cheese and 2 tablespoons Parmesan cheese on top and cook in 350 degree oven until cheese is melted and bubbles. Serve with extra sauce if you like. We like this with a big salad and garlic bread.

Michael T. Hughes

Mike Hughes is the executive director of Prehab of Arizona in Mesa. A former special education teacher, he is actively involved in many community programs, including East Valley Boys and Girls Club, Kiwanis of the Superstitions, City of Mesa Gang Control Steering Committee, Mesa United Way Management Assistance Program, Mesa Public Schools Appeals Board and is the President of the Board of Directors for Family Life Center. Mike is a Mesa Leadership Alumni member and coaches basketball at the Mesa YMCA.

OLD FASHIONED HOMEMADE CABBAGE BURGERS

**1 lg. head of cabbage, diced, steamed to soften
(10-15 minutes), drained
1 lb. ground beef, browned
1 med. onion, diced and sautéed
salt and pepper to taste
hot roll mix or refrigerator rolls
melted butter**

Mix cabbage with beef and onion and refrigerate.

Prepare hot roll mix for dough or use refrigerator rolls. Roll dough out long. Cut into roll size strips. Fill with cabbage mixture. Cover with top strip. Pinch sides together all the way around. Place on greased baking sheet—not touching. Brush top with melted butter before and after baking. Bake at 375 degrees for 15 to 20 minutes or until browned nicely.

Eugene M. Hughes

Eugene M. Hughes

Eugene M. Hughes is the former president of Northern Arizona University in Flagstaff. He chairs the American Association of State Colleges and Universities; was 1992-1993 president of the Arizona State Board of Education; commissioner, Western Interstate Commission on Higher Education; is chair of the Arizona Leadership Advisory Council; is a member of the Governor's Strategic Partnership for Economic Development; and is a charter member of the NCAA (National Collegiate Athletic Association) President's Commission. He has also served as a member of the board of directors of the Flagstaff Festival of the Arts; president of the Flagstaff East Rotary Club; member of the board of directors of the Flagstaff Chamber of Commerce; the board of trustees for the Museum of Northern Arizona; and the executive board of the Grand Canyon Council —Boy Scouts of America. In 1988, Mr. Hughes was named "Flagstaff Citizen of the Year".

HERB STUFFED PORK CHOPS WITH WINE SAUCE

6 double pork chops
salt and pepper to taste
1/4 C. butter
3/4 C. chopped onion
1/4 C. chopped celery
1 1/2 C. bread cubes
1 tsp. crushed fennel seeds
1/2 C. chopped parsley
dry white wine
1 tsp. cornstarch for each cup of liquid to be thickened

Have the butcher cut pockets in the pork chops. Preheat oven to 350 degrees. Sprinkle chops inside and out with salt and pepper. Heat 3 tablespoons of the butter and sauté onion and celery. Add bread cubes, seeds and parsley and stuff chops. Fasten with toothpicks.

In a skillet or dutch oven, add the other tablespoon of butter and brown chops on both sides. Add wine to a depth of 1/4"; cover and bake one hour, or until tender.

Transfer chops to a warm platter. Bring sauce to boil. Mix cornstarch with a little water and thicken sauce.

Everyone loves this dish!

Bev Hermon

Bev Hermon of Tempe is an Arizona state senator representing District 17. The 41st Arizona Legislature (1993-1994) Directory lists her occupation as former educator. Committee assignments are: Education, Chair; Judiciary, Vice Chair; Appropriations; Government.

SPAGHETTI PIE

6 oz. spaghetti
2 Tbsp. butter or margarine
1/3 C. grated Parmesan cheese
2 well-beaten eggs
1 C. sour cream
1 lb. ground beef or bulk pork sausage
1/2 C. chopped onion
1/4 C. chopped green pepper
1 - 8 oz. can (1 cup) tomatoes, cut up
1 - 6 oz. can tomato paste
1 tsp. sugar
1 tsp. dried oregano, crushed
1/2 tsp. garlic salt
1/2 C. shredded mozzarella cheese (2 oz.)

Cook the spaghetti according to package directions; drain (should have about 3 cups spaghetti). Stir butter or margarine into hot spaghetti. Stir in Parmesan cheese and eggs. Form spaghetti mixture into a "crust" in a buttered 10-inch pie plate. Spread sour cream over bottom of spaghetti crust.

In skillet cook ground beef or pork sausage, onion, and green pepper until vegetables are tender and meat is browned. Drain off excess fat. Stir in undrained tomatoes, tomato paste, sugar, oregano, an garlic salt; heat through.

Turn meat mixture into spaghetti crust. Bake, uncovered, in 350 degree oven for 20 minutes. Sprinkle the mozzarella cheese on top. Bake 5 minutes longer or until cheese melts.

Yield: Serves 6.

Warren J. Iliff

Warren J. Iliff is the executive director of The Phoenix Zoo in Papago Park.

SESAME GINGER CHICKEN

1 Tbsp. sesame seeds, toasted
2 Tbsp. peeled, grated ginger root
2 Tbsp. honey
2 Tbsp. soy sauce
4 boned, skinned chicken breast halves
thin green onion strips

Combine first four ingredients in small bowl. Stir well and set aside. Flatten each chicken breast to 1/4 inches thick. Coat grill rack with cooking spray. Place on grill, basting frequently with soy sauce mixture, until done. Place chicken on serving platter, garnish with green onion strips.

Yield: Serves 4.

Opal H. Johnson

Opal H. Johnson

Opal Johnson is the 1991 Mesa Woman of the Year. Opal has lived in Mesa for 30-plus years working as a journalist and volunteering her services to her community. She served on Mesa Community Council, Mesa Public Library Board, Mesa United Way Board of Directors, Mental Health Association Board of Directors, Project Mobility Board President, and Sirrine Day Care Auxiliary Board to mention a few. And she dreams of parachuting out of an airplane for kicks on her 80th birthday this year!

CHICKEN CONTINENTAL

6 to 8 chicken breasts (always use with bones/skin)
1/2 stick butter
3 cans cream of chicken soup
salt to taste
3 Tbsp. (heaping) celery flakes
2 Tbsp. rubbed thyme
2 C. cooked brown rice (can mix with yellow)

Sauté chicken breast in butter until tender. Remove breast from skillet, add soup to drippings and combine well. Add salt, celery flakes, and thyme. Combine well and add rice. Place breast in glass dish and cover with mixture. Bake 30 minutes at 350 degrees.

Naomi Judd

Naomi Judd

The Judd's are famous country and western singers. (Author's note: I solicited their recipe because one of their videos was taped in Sedona.) Naomi, the mom, wrote: *"This is Wynonna's favorite dish! It's what I fix when she comes home off the road. She likes it with steamed zucchini, yeast rolls and cherry jello fruit salad."*

ONE DISH STEAK AND POTATOES

Cut desired amount of **round steak** into 2" x 2" squares. Brown and season then place across bottom of baking dish.

Slice **peeled potatoes** (seasoning each layer) over meat ending with a thick layer of **onion (about 1/2 onion).** Set aside.

Add water to browning pan, stirring to release meat juices. Bring liquid to simmer then add **1 tsp. beef bouillon** and/or **Kitchen Bouquet®.** Simmer two minutes stirring constantly then pour into side of meat/potato/onion dish. (Liquid level should be about 1 1/2" from baking dish rim). Cover with foil and bake at 350 degrees for 1 1/2 to 2 hours.

Remove liquid and thicken for gravy. Pour over top of steak/potatoes and serve.

Note: If round steak is coated with a thick layer of flour before browning, liquid may be thickened in baking dish providing it's own gravy.

Jimmy V. Judd

Jimmy V. Judd is the sheriff of Cochise County in Bisbee.

SAVORY CRESCENT CHICKEN SQUARES

3 oz. pkg.cream cheese, softened	2 Tbsp. milk
3 Tbsp. butter, melted	1 Tbsp. chopped onions
2 C. cooked chicken	8 oz. Pillsbury® refrigerated crescent dough
1/4 tsp. salt	3/4 cup seasoned croutons, crushed
1/8 tsp. pepper	

Preheat over to 350 degrees. In medium bowl, mix cream cheese and two tablespoons butter, reserving one tablespoon of butter until smooth. Add the next five ingredients and mix well.

Separate the dough into four rectangles. Take the chicken mixture and spread evenly in the center of each rectangle. Fold the dough over and crease the edges. Take one tablespoon of butter and spread on top of the squares, then sprinkle with crushed croutons. Bake until lightly brown.

Paul Johnson

Paul Johnson is the mayor of the city of Phoenix.

KASHA CASSEROLE

In large pot combine:
1 1/2 C. kasha (roasted buckwheat groats)
6 to 8 C. water
1 chopped onion
1 chopped carrot
2 C. mixed vegetables (broccoli & green beans work well)

Bring to boil. Cover and cook about 10 minutes on medium flame, stirring occasionally. Check water level. When most of water is absorbed, add:

4 to 6 oz. cubed cheese
1/4 C. peanut butter
1 egg
1\4 C. wheat germ
1/4 C. whole wheat flour
1/4 to 1/2 C. tamari/soy sauce

Mix it all up and bake in greased casserole dish at 350 degrees for 30 minutes. Enjoy!

Rabbi Bonnie Koppell

Rabbi Bonnie J. Koppell

Rabbi Bonnie Koppell is the spiritual leader at Temple Beth Sholom. She became the first female rabbi ever to serve in the military. In November, 1992, she became the first female rabbi promoted to the rank of major. She was quoted as saying, "*Although patriotism was not a motivation for my going into the military, it is a motivation for my staying. I feel very fortunate to live in America, and if I can pay back a little of that debt, then it's worth the time I give to it.*" In addition to her reserve and religious work, Koppell serves on the Resource Distribution Committee for the Mesa United Way and was a member of the process management committee for Downtown Mesa Tomorrow.

CHICKEN ON SUNDAY

1 or 2 cups Minute® Rice
1 can cream of mushroom soup
1 can cream of celery soup
1/2 cup or 1 can evaporated milk
1 can water chestnuts drained (optional)
4 split chicken breasts
1 envelope Lipton® Dry Onion Soup Mix

Grease 9 x 13 baking pan. Sprinkle rice on bottom of pan. Heat mushroom and celery soups, milk, and water chestnuts and pour over rice. Lay chicken breasts on top of rice mixture. Sprinkle with onion soup mix to cover chicken. Seal pan with aluminum foil. Bake 2 hours 15 minutes at 350 degrees.

Kevin Leman

Kevin Leman is an internationally-known psychologist, radio and television personality, and speaker. Dr. Leman has entertained audiences worldwide with his wit and common sense psychology. He has appeared on numerous radio and television programs including: "Oprah Winfrey", "Donahue", "Sally Jessy Raphael", "Good Morning America", "Live with Regis and Kathie Lee", "Jenny Jones", "Joan Rivers", "CBS This Morning", and "The Today Show". Dr. Leman is the co-host of the nationally-syndicated radio show, "Parent-Talk" — the nation's first live talk show where parents talk to parents. Dr. Leman has about a dozen best-selling books with a new one on the way entitled *Bringing Up Kids Without Tearing Them Down*. Originally from New York, he and his wife, Sande, live in Tucson with their five children.

SCAMPI E CAPE SANTE ALLA GRIGLIA
(Broiled Shrimp & Scallops)

1 lb. medium shrimp
1 lb. scallops
1/2 C. olive oil
1/3 C. chopped parsley
3 garlic cloves, finely
    chopped

1/2 C. dry unflavored
    bread crumbs
salt to taste
freshly ground pepper to taste
lemon wedges

Shell and devein shrimp. Wash shrimp and scallops under cold running water. Pat dry with paper towels. In a large bowl, combine oil, parsley, garlic, bread crumbs and salt and pepper. Add shrimp and scallops to mixture. Mix until well coated. Let stand 1 hour. Preheat broiler. Remove shrimp and scallops from marinade. Gently press some extra bread crumb mixture onto shrimp and scallops. Place alternately on 4 to 6 metal skewers. Put skewers under hot broiler. Broil 2 minutes or until golden. Turn skewers over and broil on the other side 2 minutes or until golden. Serve immediately with lemon wedges. Whether you serve this dish as an appetizer or main course, it is equally sensational.

Daniel A. Luciano

Dan Luciano is the general manager for the Phoenix Greyhound Park. In November, 1992, he was named general manager of American Greyhound Racing Inc., which operates dog tracks in Phoenix and Apache Junction. Mr. Luciano was quoted in the newspaper as saying, *"I see the dogs as our stars. If we protect them, take care of them, it will benefit everyone"*. One of the first things he did as general manager was to draw up new contracts on behalf of the dogs to stipulate specifically where the dogs will go after their racing days have ended. He said, *"The only acceptable destination to us is to another racetrack, to its original owner or to an approved adoption program."*

MEXICAN QUICHE

1 - 6 inch flour tortillas
3/4 C. Jack cheese (4 oz.)
6 oz. bulk pork sausage
2 Tbsp. chopped green pepper
2 eggs
1/2 C. milk or light cream
1/8 tsp. salt
hot salsa (optional)
fresh cilantro (optional)

Starting with a cold skillet, heat tortillas about 45 seconds, or until warm, turning once. Place tortillas into a greased 15 ounce casserole. Top with 1/2 of cheese. In the same skillet, cook sausage and green pepper until sausage is crisp tender; drain well. Spoon over tortillas and cheese in casserole. In a small bowl, combine eggs, milk or cream, and salt. Mix well. Pour egg mixture into casserole. Top with remaining cheese. Bake in 350 degree oven for 30 to 35 minutes or until firm. Serve with hot salsa and cilantro, if desired.

Yield: Makes 2 quiches.

Donald J. Logue

Donald J. Logue is the chief executive officer of Lewis R. Pyle Memorial Hospital in Payson. He has been in the hospital business for 33 years. Sixteen years were spent at Kingman Regional as president and CEO. He was activated for Desert Storm in December of 1990 and stayed in the Army for six months. Logue recently visited Russia and found an 8-year-old boy with thyroid cancer, among the most rare of all cancers and very uncommon for children. The boy is a victim of the 1986 disaster at Chernobyl. A Russian doctor asked Dr. Logue if he could treat the child because they didn't have the capabilities. Logue arranged for this child to be brought to the Children's Hospital, and the boy's aunt and physician stayed with Logue and his wife during the boy's stay. Children's Hospital treated the boy for free.

ENCHILADAS VALLARTA

PICO DE GALLO FILLING
2 lg. tomatoes, diced
1 lg. onion, diced
5 med. jalapeño peppers, diced
1 C. chopped cilantro leaves
1/4 tsp. salt
1/4 tsp. pepper
1/4 tsp. coriander
1 Tbsp. lime juice
ENCHILADAS
12 med. flour tortillas
4 C. shredded Jack cheese
1 can (27 oz.) enchilada sauce

Construction of enchilada:

Combine Pico De Gallo ingredients. Spoon equal amounts of cheese and salsa into each tortilla. Roll tortillas to form enchiladas. Place tightly together in large baking dish. Pour enchilada sauce over enchiladas. Bake in 350 degree oven for 30 minutes. Makes 12 delicious and spicy enchiladas! Enjoy!

Veronica L. Newth

Veronica L. Newth

Veronica Newth is "Miss Teen Arizona 1983". This is an original recipe from Veronica who is strictly vegetarian.

SOUTHWEST CHILI DELIGHT

"This was my favorite school lunch when I was in the 3rd grade . . ."

Place **1/2 cup of regular (not dip Size) Fritos® Corn Chips** in a bowl. Fill bowl with your favorite (steaming hot!) **chili con carne**. Quickly add **1/4 inch layer of grated longhorn chedder cheese** on top of the chili. Add a **dollop of sour cream** to the center of the now melted cheese. Eat before Fritos become soggy!

Hans Olson

Hans Olson

Hans Olson is a local legend who has been playing his harmonica and guitar in Arizona since 1969. Olson's music is hard to categorize, though a blues flavor dominates with added folk, rock and country making it his own personal blend. *You Wish* is an eleven year old recording of his, and you may have heard his harmonica in TV's "Evening Shade" in the first season as the opening theme. He recently released *Where's the Grey,* and will be doing a couple of demo projects that will probably be for sale.

CHICKEN GINGER ROGERS

2 chicken breasts, boneless and skinless
olive oil
2 green onions, french cut
2 cloves of garlic, pressed
lemon and fresh ginger root pieces, thinly sliced
1/2 C. white wine or beer
1/4 C. low salt soy sauce
dash five-spice powder
cayenne

Sauté chicken breasts in olive oil until lightly browned. Don't overcook. Remove and set aside. Add onions and cloves of garlic and sauté these lightly. Replace chicken breasts and cover with lemon and ginger root pieces. Add white wine or beer, soy sauce, five-spice powder and cayenne. Cover and simmer for about 20 minutes or until the bouquet of herbs and spices are well mixed. Serve with fresh pasta or brown rice and a fresh garden salad.

R. Carlos Nakai (signature)

R. Carlos Nakai

Carlos Nakai, a native of Flagstaff, began playing the Native American flute in 1973, after earlier music studies on the classical trumpet at Northern Arizona University. The flute traditionally has been used for courting and healing. He mastered the traditional flute tunes and blended in his own ideas to create a style of his own — still honoring tradition and developing new expressions. Nakai was born in Flagstaff in 1946. Early in his life, as a Navajo-Ute, he became interested in the culture of his people and other North American tribes. *Changes, Earth Spirit, Journeys, Spirit Horse,* and *Canyon Trilogy* are a few of his recordings. *Cycles* is the music track for the Heard Museum multi-media presentation, *Our Voices, Our Land,* which features Native American flute and synthesizer. Nakai also is the founder of the ethnic jazz ensemble, Jackalope, which has released two albums, *Jackalope* and *Weavings.*

CHINESE CHILE PORK

3 to 5 dry black Chinese mushrooms, sliced thin
2 pork steaks, sliced thin into strips
1 piece preserved Chinese radish (I bought this canned,
    already shredded at a Chinese store. The more you
    use, the stronger the salt and chile flavor)
salt
2 to 4 Tbsp. soy sauce, depending on amount of pork used
1 to 2 Tbsp. flour, depending on amount of pork used

Soak mushrooms in warm water until soft (about 30 minutes). Put sliced pork in pie pan. Add Chinese radish strips. Sprinkle all with a little salt.

Moisten mixture with soy sauce. Mix in flour. Gently press water out of mushrooms and slice into thin strips; add and mix all ingredients and spread out in pan.

Steam until pork is done. Serve with white rice and a vegetable dish. This dish has a strong flavor and will encourage consumption of rice. I try to prepare another dish that has fresh vegetables and a milder flavor to serve in addition to this.

Rosalind Onodera

Rosalind Ong Onodera

Rosalind Onadera of Phoenix is a member of Pacific Rim Advisory Council, Chinese American Citizens Alliance, and Arizona Asian American Association. Rosalind solicited some helpful hints from her mom and husband to deviate from the original recipe. She said water chestnuts would add some "crunch" and chunks of eggplant would be good to experiment with. Her husband suggested shredded cabbage but she thinks it would be great stir-fried on the side but not steamed along with the pork. But you have to consider her husband was watching football when he made the suggestion and maybe he wasn't concentrating as much on recipes as he was on wide receivers!

BUFFALO ROUND STEAK

Round steak can be fried, chicken-fried, baked or done on the grill. It should not be broiled, because, like broiled beef round steak, it will be tough.

A favorite way to prepare **round steak** is to cut the meat in serving size pieces, dip them in **beaten egg** and then in finely **crushed bread** or **cracker crumbs** and brown in **hot oil** in a skillet. Place in a baking dish. Add 1 to 2 cups water to browning skillet and pour over steak. Cover with foil. Bake at 250 degrees approximately 2 hours per pound. **Salt and pepper to taste**.

Note: The amount of water needed will depend on how big a batch you are making. A 9 x 13 pan that is full will need 3-4 cups of water.

Gemmie Baker

Gemmie Baker is the owner of the Buffalo Museum of America located in Scottsdale. The museum was established as a tribute to these great animals and is a culmination of many years of personal research and collecting by Gemmie. His full-size buffalo model was used as a prop in the award-winning film *Dances With Wolves*. In the 1900's the nation's buffalo population was on the verge of extinction, but today approximately 90 to 95 thousand buffalo live in refuges and ranches throughout the western United States.

CHILES RELLENOS CON QUESO

Green Chiles—skin, cut lengthwise, remove seeds (insert
   fingersize piece of cheese into chile and close)
For every 2 chiles use 1 egg. Separate yolks from whites.

   For 6 yolks:
1 tsp. baking powder
1 tsp. salt
2 Tbsp. cream

   Beat and add:
1 Tbsp. flour.

   Whip and fold in whites. Heat oil in skillet. Add batter in shape of chilie, add chilie (cut side down). Cover with batter, turn, and brown. Serve with salsa or enchilada sauce.

Joy Fox

Joy Fox McGrew

   Joy Fox is a ceramic sculptor whose exhibits have appeared in numerous Arizona museums, galleries, and publications. Fox has also exhibited her art in New York City, Nevada, California, Kansas, Pennsylvania, Mexico, and Scotland. A very exciting aspect of her life has been living in the foothills of Arizona's Santa Catalina Mountains, about an hour's drive north of Tucson, on an old dude ranch called Rancho Linda Vista.   In 1968, a group of 11 families bought the ranch with the idea of forming a "community of the arts". Today, the ranch's 42 residents, most of whom are writers, artists and craftsmen, enjoy an environment they find conducive to artistic endeavors. Joy prepares for her work by exploring the landscape and gathering visual information which once back in the studio she translates into clay sculptures and paintings. In 1993, the families celebrated their 25th anniversary at the ranch near the village of Oracle.

CHICKEN OR TURKEY CASSEROLE

1 med. zucchini squash, chopped
4 carrots, diced
1 sm. onion, chopped
2 Tbsp. margarine or butter

Steam all the above for about 30 minutes or until squash is translucent.

Mix together in bowl:

1 can cream of chicken soup
8 oz. sour cream
2 C. chunks of chicken or turkey. (You can use leftover chicken or turkey or you can use large cans of boneless chicken or turkey.)
2 C. shredded cheddar cheese.

Mix 1 package chicken-flavored Stove Top® Stuffing per instructions.

In 9 x 13 pan or dish, line bottom of pan with vegetables, then chicken or turkey mixture and top with stuffing. Heat in oven 20-25 minutes. It can also be heated in the microwave.

Can be served with cranberries and pumpkin pie and have a Thanksgiving dinner any time of the year.

Ralph Pomeroy

Ralph Pomeroy is the superintendent of Queen Creek Unified School District.

SALSA DI NINA PIERO

2 lg. red onions, chopped
5 to 6 cloves of garlic
1/3 C. olive oil (extra virgin)
1 - 5 lb. deboned and tied pork roast
4 lg. cans crushed Italian Roma tomatoes
1 lg. can tomato paste
2 lg. cans tomato sauce
2 bay leaves
1 Tbsp. pure white cane sugar
1 Tbsp. red wine vinegar

In large saucepan, mix red onions, cut fresh garlic cloves, add olive oil, then place pork roast in pan. Brown onions, garlic and pork roast. Remove roast. Pour in 4 cans of large crushed Italian Roma tomatoes, 1 can of tomato paste and from the same can of paste, add equal amount of water. Add tomato sauce, bay leaves, pure white cane sugar and red wine vinegar. Gently place the 5 pound pork roast back in the same pan. Salt and pepper to taste. Simmer for 6 hours turning and gently stirring the sauce every 15 or 20 minutes.

Pour over pasta of choice and over the sliced pork roast.

Buon Appetito!

Perry Damone

Perry Damone is a radio broadcaster for KEZ 99.9 FM in Phoenix. Perry helped start the youngest run radio station in the world: 6th graders' KdSTR (590 AM) in Chandler at Shumay Elementary, which has been named the No. 1 educational program in the country. Perry was born in Los Angeles, California, and was raised by his father, Vic Damone, and his mother, Anna Maria Pierangeli, in Italy. They moved back to the United States in 1967 and at age 12 Perry learned how to speak English through Los Angeles area radio broadcasters. He was educated in Rome, Paris, and London, and he is fluent in Italian, French, and English. He enjoys travel, music, golf, promotions, and has recently added cooking to his list of interests.

BEEF WITH BROCCOLI

"The ingredient quantities are approximate. I never measure any quantities while cooking any meal. This recipe can be adjusted for any taste except for former President Bush who does not care for broccoli."

2 C. broccoli
2 Tbsp. sugar
1 Tbsp. corn starch
1 C. water
1/4 C. soy sauce
1 C. thin sliced beef
cooking oil

Cut broccoli into 1-inch size. Mix sugar, corn starch, water and soy sauce together in a bowl.

Heat cooking oil in frying pan, add the broccoli and stir fry for 3 to 4 minutes. Remove the broccoli and set aside.

Heat cooking oil again and stir fry the sliced beef for 1 to 2 minutes.

After stir frying the meat, add the sauce to the meat in the pan and allow the sauce to boil for 15 to 20 seconds, then add the broccoli and mix together.

Pour the broccoli and beef onto a bed of rice and serve.

Willie Wong

Willie Wong

Willie Wong is the mayor of the city of Mesa. He was the first Chinese-American mayor elected in the United States.

SPANISH QUICHE

1 can Pillsbury® crescent rolls
1 small onion, diced
3 strips bacon, fried and crumbled (about 1/2 cup)
1/2 cup ham, diced
8 oz. mozzarella, 6 oz. Swiss, 6 oz. Jack cheese, shredded
salt and pepper to taste
dry parsley, sprinkled on top
1 egg, beaten in measuring cup with
    enough half & half to almost fill cup.

Press crescent rolls into cookie sheet, ridge edges. Spread with the onion, bacon, ham, cheeses, salt, pepper and parsley. Top with egg mixture. Bake at 350 for 20-25 minutes.

This is a great main dish for lunch or dinner when served with a salad or it can be cut to small pieces for a party appetizer.

Keven Willey

Keven Willey

Keven Willey is a political columnist for *The Arizona Republic*. (Author's note: A friend of mine, Peggy DiGuisto, had to do a shadowing as part of her graduation requirements for Mesa Leadership Training and Development. Peggy chose Keven to shadow for a day and had a very exciting experience. Peggy was kind enough to solicit a recipe from Keven for this cookbook so I want to thank both Keven and Peggy for their contributions.)

HAMBURGER-RICE PIE

Cook in skillet until brown:
1/4 C. butter
1 1/3 C. Minute® Rice
1/2 C. chopped onion
1/4 C. chopped green pepper

Add:
1 bouillon cube
2 2/3 C. water
1 tsp. sugar
1/2 tsp. salt
1 1/3 sm. can tomato sauce

Mix lightly. Simmer 15 minutes covered, no stirring.

Combine:
1 lb. hamburger
1 tsp. salt
2/3 C. tomato sauce
1/4 C. chopped onion
1/2 C. bread crumbs
dash garlic powder

Mix well. Press firmly on bottom and sides of 9 x 12 pan. Turn cooked rice mixture into meat shell. Sprinkle 1/2 cup grated cheese over top.

Bake in 350 degree oven for 25 minutes. Serve hot.

☺

Keith Vaughan

Keith Vaughan is the principal at Gilbert High School.

TROUT LOFTFIELD

(In honor of our Norwegian ancestors)

1 fresh trout
olive oil
lemon juice
cayenne pepper
salt
thyme
1 to 2 strips bacon
caraway seed

Rub each cleaned trout inside and out with olive oil. Sprinkle liberally inside and out with remaining ingredients. Cover and refrigerate from 8 to 24 hours. Wrap 1 to 2 bacon strips around trout and grill on a greased grill—ten minutes on one side and 15 on the other.

Kate Ruland-Thorne (signature)

Kate Ruland-Thorne

Kate Ruland-Thorne is the first woman editor of the *Sedona Red Rock News*, and *Sedona Magazine & Visitors' Guide*; author of *Lion Of Redstone*, *Experience Sedona Legends and Legacies*, co-author of *Experience Jerome* and *The Verde Valley Legends and Legacies*; *Adventures in Arizona: An Illustrated History*. Kate specializes in information on Sedona, artist profiles and art subjects; biography, and regional history. She is currently serving as president of the Sedona Historical Society; publicity chairman for Western American Week; was co-founder and first president of Arizona Indian Living Treasure Awards; and in 1989 formed her own publishing company, Thorne Enterprises Publications, Inc., with her husband Keith and son Reed for the purpose of publishing recreational maps and regional histories. Recently she was admitted into Who's Who International.

STUFFED PORK CHOPS

4 thick pork chops, 1 1/2 inches

    FILLING
2 apples, unpeeled, cored, chopped
1/2 C. raisins
3/4 C. fresh bread crumbs (from French bread)
1 Tbsp. brown sugar
1/2 tsp. each—black pepper, salt and ground cloves
2 Tbsp. each—melted butter, chopped chives or parsley
2 Tbsp. butter or margarine
1 C. beef broth

    Trim excess fat from pork chops. Make slit to form a pocket in fat end of each pork chop. In bowl, combine apples, raisins, bread crumbs, brown sugar, pepper, salt and cloves. Add melted butter and chives or parsley. Mix well. Let stand for a few minutes for flavors to blend. Stuff each pork chop with generous portion of stuffing. Skewer shut with toothpicks. Heat butter in heavy skillet. Brown chops slowly over medium heat, about 5 minutes on each side. Add beef broth. Bring to a simmer. Simmer pork chops over low to medium heat for about 30 minutes or until tender. Remove toothpicks. Transfer to serving platter. Pour pan juices over pork chops and serve immediately with a green salad and steamed broccoli.

    TIP: Be sure to simmer pork chops over low to medium heat rather than over high heat on the stove in order to keep them tender.

Robert H. Tippett

Robert H. Tippett is the mayor of the city of Yuma.

JAMBALAYA

1/4 C. cooking oil	1 tsp. thyme
1/2 lb. smoked sausage, sliced	1 tsp. black pepper
1/2 lb. ham, cubed	1/4 tsp. cayenne pepper
1/2 lb. chicken, cut up in chunks	1 tsp. salt
1 C. onion, chopped	1 C. long grain rice
1 C. bell pepper, chopped	1 1/2 C. stock or water
1 C. celery, chopped	1 1/2 Tbsp. Worcestershire
2 clove garlic, minced	sauce
1 can (14 1/2 oz.) tomatoes, drained, reserving liquid	1 1/2 lbs. peeled raw shrimp

In a large Dutch oven, sauté sausage, ham and chicken in oil until lightly browned. Remove from pot. Sauté onions, celery, bell peppers and garlic in meat drippings until tender. Add tomatoes, thyme, black and cayenne pepper and salt. Cook 5 minutes. Stir in rice. Mix together liquid from tomatoes, stock and Worcestershire sauce to equal 2 1/2 cups. Pour into the pot. Bring to a boil, reduce to a simmer. Add raw shrimp, ham, sausage and chicken. Cook uncovered, stirring occasionally for about 30 minutes or until rice and shrimp are done.

Yield: 4 to 6 servings.

Daniel H. Taylor
Martha Taylor

Dan & Martha Taylor

Dan and Martha Taylor both work in the aging field and are advocates for the elderly. Dan is the executive director at the Mesa Senior Center and Martha is the project director for Retired Seniors Volunteer Program (RSVP) in Tempe serving the East Valley. Both are graduates of the Mesa Leadership Training and Development Program sponsored by the Mesa Chamber of Commerce. Dan and Martha serve on various boards and are especially interested in working with projects involving seniors.

ANN & FIFE'S LASAGNE

2 lbs. extra lean ground beef
1 lg. onion, chopped
1 clove garlic, minced
6 bay leaves

salt and pepper
1 can (12 oz.) tomato paste
2 cans (12 oz.) water

Cook above ingredients together slowly, at least 1 hour (about #3 on electric range) Remove bay leaves. Twenty minutes before meat is done, cook **12 lasagne** noodles as directed on package. Rinse in cold water; keep in water until ready to use. Place 6 noodles in 16 x 11 x 2 glass dish. On top of noodles put 1/2 of sauce, **1 cup cottage cheese, 1/4 cup fresh grated Parmesan cheese** and **1/2 pound grated mozzarella cheese**. Start with noodles and repeat. Cover with foil, place on cookie sheet and bake in 350 degree oven for 45 minutes. Let rest at least 20 minutes before serving.

Yield: 12 servings.

Ann & Fife Symington

Fife Symington is the governor of Arizona. Ann Symington is the first lady of Arizona.

STUMP FARMS PIT BARBECUE

Pre-Heat Pit Oven:

Dig a hole 4 feet wide, 4 feet deep and 6 feet long. Fill the hole with mesquite or other hardwood. Light the fire approximately 4-6 hours prior to use. It should be burned down after this time to leave a bed of coals at least 2-3 feet deep.

Meat Preparation:

Take **10—10 pound chunks of boneless chuck** or any type of boneless meat. Season with **Morton® Sugar Cure** by rubbing liberally onto the meat. Place each chunk in a **microwave turkey bag**. Make sure it is sealed to retain the juice as the meat is cooked, then wrap in **plain butcher paper** and place in a **damp burlap sack** (available at any feed store). Tie tightly with wire. Have all sacks ready before placing any in the pit oven.

Barbecue:

Rapidly, place all damp burlap meat packages directly on top of the coals. Cover the meat with a piece of tin, and then very quickly cover with 3 feet of dirt. Make sure dirt is tromped down firmly so that no heat escapes.

Bake for 24-30 hours. Dig up and serve with your favorite salsa, BBQ sauce, tortillas, pinto beans or coleslaw.

Yield: 200 servings.

Bob Stump

Bob Stump represents Arizona in District 3 in the United States House of Representatives.

ROAULADDE

A German dish from Grandma Mitch and Aunt Jean Schultz

round steak   •   bacon   •   onions

MEAT: Slice round steak as thin as possible. Trim off excess fat and cut into pieces approximately 4 by 4 inches. Lightly salt.

STUFFING: With scissors cut bacon into small bits. Chop onions and mix in equal proportions with bacon.

PREPARATION: With each piece of meat, place generous portion of stuffing on the meat. Roll meat like stuffed cabbage and tie around with string to hold together. Toothpicks may also be used to hold meat together.

COOKING: Oil bottom of large frying pan and brown the excess pieces of meat that have been trimmed away. Throw out the meat. Then brown the rolled pieces of meat in that pan. Place browned pieces of meat in large cooking pan. Cover rolled pieces with the oil from the pan. Add water to the pan until just shy of covering all of the meat. Bake in 350 degree oven for approximately 2 hours. Remove from oven and let stand for several hours.

SERVE: Remove meat from pan. Mix flour with juices from pan to make gravy. Heat meat and eat!

Buddy Schultz

Buddy Schultz was a pitcher who played with the Chicago Cubs and St. Louis Cardinals from 1975-1980. He is a graduate of Miami University in Oxford, Ohio, where he holds the NCAA record for strikeouts in one 9 inning game, 26. He was drafted by the Cubs in 1972 and recorded a victory in his first Major League appearance. He currently lives in Scottsdale and is married with 2 children. He is the president of his own company—Most Valuable Promotions.

NO-RECIPE TERIYAKI CHICKEN

O.K., I can't cook. I can't even follow a recipe. I don't know, it's just all those 1/4's and 1/2's that scare me away. I do like a Teriyaki Chicken dish that my wife makes, so I asked her to give me the recipe. She said, "I don't have one. I just do it." So I said, "Well, just tell me how to do it, but leave off all the 1/2's and 1/4's." So, she did and here it is . . .

Put **eight boneless, skinless frozen chicken breasts** in large-sized casserole dish that has a cover. (Don't put the cover on yet.)

Hold a bottle of **white vinegar** in one hand and a bottle of **low-salt soy sauce** in the other and dump in equal amounts until you just cover the chicken breasts. (I noticed when you do this, little parts of the chicken breasts will be peeking out from under the surface of the brown liquid mixture like rocks in a flowing river.)

Sprinkle **garlic powder** over the liquid mixture in the dish so it completely covers the surface of liquid. (It kind of looks like sawdust floating on water wall-to-wall in a pot.)

Now you can cover the casserole dish and put it in the oven at 300 degrees for at least 3 hours. (Seems like a long time, but it makes those chicken breasts so tender and juicy that they almost fall apart.)

Cook a pot full of rice, drain off the water and put some on a big plate. Then put a piece of chicken on the rice and splash some of the brown sauce around.

E.A. Smith, M.D.

Edward A. Smith

Ed Smith is a physician specializing in internal medicine and preventive medicine in his Diagnostic Clinic in Mesa. He also writes a column for the Tribune Newspapers that is distributed nationally across the Cox and New York Times wire services. (Author's note: Dr. Smith's recipe arrived in the mailbox with bits of rice falling out of the envelope, which itself was stained with soy sauce. What a character!)

WONDERFUL VEGETABLE ENCHILADAS

1 zucchini squash
1 gold bar squash
1 summer squash
1 med. sweet onion
1 carton (8 oz.) low fat
    ricotta cheese
2 tsp. flour
2 tsp. Crisco®

2 cans enchilada sauce
lemon pepper
garlic salt
onion salt
1 pkg. corn tortillas
2 C. grated cheese
    (your favorite)

Cut up squash to bite size and microwave for 3 minutes or until slightly done. Dice onion (whole or half) and put in bowl with ricotta cheese. While the squash is cooking, make sauce by browning flour and Crisco in saucepan, then adding the enchilada sauce (about 1 1/2 cans) and about 1/2 can water. Stir and bring to boil, then turn off heat and let sit on burner.

Take vegetables out of microwave and put in bowl with onion and ricotta cheese. Add dash of lemon pepper, garlic salt and onion salt for taste. Mix.

Take corn tortillas and dip one at a time in sauce mixture and place in cake pan. Add vegetable filling and grated cheese and roll, placing each enchilada next to each other. Use remaining sauce and pour over the top and add grated cheese. Bake in 350 degree oven until lightly browned and cheese is melted.

Yield: 12 to 24 enchiladas, depending on amount of filling.

Mark Schnepf

Mark Schnepf

Mark Schnepf is the mayor of the town of Queen Creek. Aside from his duties as mayor and tending to his family-owned farm, Mark is active in numerous organizations and is on the Prehab Board of Directors.

CHICKEN SAUTÉED IN WINE & GINGER SAUCE

1 lg. can chicken broth
3 - 3 1/2 lb. chicken pieces
2 tsp. salt
1/4 tsp. pepper
3 Tbsp. butter
1/2 C. white wine vinegar
1/8 tsp. nutmeg
1/8 tsp. cinnamon
1/8 tsp. ginger
2 egg yolks

Simmer chicken pieces in broth, salt and pepper until tender. Melt butter in large skillet, arrange the pieces of chicken so that they don't overlap and brown on both sides. Put 3/4 cup of the broth, the vinegar and the rest of the seasonings into a small saucepan and bring to a boil. Lower heat and simmer for 10 minutes. Remove from heat, stir in egg yolks and return to heat. Simmer until sauce thickens. Pour sauce over chicken in skillet and stir to coat all pieces evenly. Arrange chicken in serving dish and pour sauce over it. Serve hot.

Jeffrey Siegel

Jeffrey Siegel is the director and producer of the Arizona Renaissance Festival in Apache Junction.

ROMLEY'S RIBS

2 slabs of baby back pork ribs (approximately 5 lbs.)

Rub the ribs lightly with salt and garlic powder. Sprinkle liberally with ground black pepper.

Place ribs on preheated outdoor grill and cook slowly for approximately 45 minutes, turning as needed. Then baste with barbecue sauce (recipe below) and continue cooking on grill for approximately 20 minutes, basting and turning frequently to keep the brown sugar in the sauce from burning.

BARBECUE SAUCE

Mix together following ingredients:
1 bottle (32 oz.) tomato ketchup
3 heaping Tbsp. prepared mustard
1/2 C. brown sugar
1/4 C. red wine vinegar
1/2 tsp. salt
2 tsp. ground black pepper
1 garlic clove, finely minced
5 drops Tabasco® sauce

Richard M. Romley

Richard Romley is the county attorney of Maricopa County.

POT ROAST GREEK STYLE

3 to 6 lbs. beef roast
1/2 tsp. salt
1 tsp. oregano
1/2 tsp. dried thyme
1/8 tsp. dry mustard
1 bay leaf, crumbled
1 to 2 cloves garlic, sliced
1 2-inch cinnamon
   stick, slivered

5 to 6 whole cloves
2 to 4 Tbsp. oil or butter
2 C. coarsely chopped canned
   tomatoes, with juice
1 can (8 oz.) tomato sauce
1/2 C. dry red wine
sm. peeled potatoes
whole peeled carrots

Rub roast with damp cloth. Rub surface of roast with salt, oregano, thyme, mustard and bay leaf. Make slits in beef in several places and insert slices of garlic, cinnamon stick slivers and cloves.

Brown roast in oil or butter in a Dutch oven, turning to brown on all sides. Add tomatoes, tomato sauce and wine. Place peeled potatoes and carrots in pan and cover. Roast in 375 degree oven for 2 1/2 to 3 hours or until done. Separate vegetables and slice meat to serve.

John Risseeuw

John Risseeuw is an associate professor of art at Arizona State University where he teaches courses in fine printing & bookmaking, papermaking, and other subjects. He also is an advisory board member of the Visual Arts Research Studios. He specializes in book arts, specifically, making books by hand and making paper by hand. His prints, books, and collaborative works have travelled in recent years in South America, Africa, Canada, England, Ireland, Germany, and Bulgaria as well as being exhibited in many cities of the United States. John's works have been featured in professional journals, and the many collections holding his work include the National Museum of American History; the New York Public Library; the Bodleian Library in Oxford, England; the Royal Family of England; and the National Baseball Hall of Fame in Cooperstown, New York, to name only a few. Formerly from Wisconsin, John has lived in Arizona since 1980.

SOUR CREAM CHICKEN ENCHILADAS

1 dozen sm. corn tortillas
1/2 C. oil
2 C. Jack cheese, shredded
3/4 C. chopped onion
1/4 C. margarine
1/4 C. flour
2 C. chicken broth
1 C. sour cream
4 oz. Ortega® chiles, chopped
2 C. cut-up chicken

Skillet-fry tortillas in oil 2 to 3 seconds on each side. Put cheese, onion and chicken in center of each. Roll up and put seam down in 13 x 9 pan.

SAUCE

Melt butter and blend flour. Add broth and cook until thick and boiling. Stir in sour cream and chiles (don't boil).

Pour over rolled enchiladas, lifting each one to get sauce underneath, too. Bake in 350 degree oven for 20 minutes. Can add additional cheese on top and bake 5 minutes more.

Tom Smith

Tom Smith

Tom Smith of Phoenix is in the Arizona House of Representatives representing District 26. The 41st Arizona Legislature (1993-1994) Directory lists his occupation as a retired educator and retired Lt. Col., USMC. Committee assignments are: Public Institutions, Chair; Appropriations; Education.

PARADISICAL PASTA

1 Tbsp. olive oil
4 garlic cloves, sliced
2 hot Italian sausages, casings removed
8 oz. mushrooms, sliced
1 bunch fresh spinach, stems trimmed
1/4 C. dry white wine
2 C. heavy cream
6 oz. Gorgonzola cheese, crumbled
2 tsp. whole grain Dijon mustard
1/2 C. toasted pine nuts or chopped walnuts
1 lb. farfalle (bowties) or fettucce (1/2 inch wide ribbons)

Heat oil in heavy skillet over medium-high heat. Add garlic and sausage, crumbling with fork and cooking until brown (about 5 minutes). Transfer sausage and garlic to bowl using slotted spoon. Add mushrooms to skillet, sauté until beginning to turn transparent. Add spinach and sauté until beginning to wilt. Add wine, cream and cheese and bring to boil, reduce heat and simmer until sauce thickens, stirring occasionally (about 10 minutes). Add sausage, mustard and nuts. Salt and pepper to taste. Stir until heated through.

Meanwhile, cook pasta in large pot of boiling water with salt and a tablespoon of olive oil until al dente. Drain, place in bowl, pour sauce over pasta and toss gently. Serves six as a first course, four as a main course.

Elin Jeffords

Elin Jeffords

Elin Jeffords is the first and longest running restaurant critic in Arizona. Elin has written for *The Arizona Republic* and was restaurant columnist, food editor and feature writer for *New Times*. As editor/author she wrote *Zagat-Arizona, Zagat-Southwest Restaurant Surveys* and *Fodor's Arizona Travel Guide 1988*. She was a restaurant reviewer for KTVK-TV in Phoenix as well as a reporter for the PM Magazine show. She has contributed to a wide variety of magazines and newspapers. In 1989 she received *The Arizona Republic's* Silver Ingot Award in appreciation of outstanding service to the newspaper and the community and in 1992, Elin was an inductee into the Arizona Culinary Hall of Fame.

POMEGRANATE-MARINATED LAMB

1 leg of lamb (5 to 6 lbs.)
8 cloves garlic, cut into slivers
1/4 C. fresh rosemary leaves
1 onion
pepper

salt
2 Tbsp. olive oil
3 C. pomegranate juice
1/2 C. red wine

Marinate lamb 1 or 2 days before cooking. Poke slits at 2-inch intervals in leg of lamb with thin knife and insert slivers of 4 or 5 garlic cloves. Combine remaining garlic cloves, rosemary, onion, pepper, salt and olive oil in food processor or blender, and puree to a paste. Rub marinade over lamb, and pour on pomegranate juice and red wine. Refrigerate, turning occasionally.

Prepare covered charcoal or gas grill. (The lamb can also be baked in the oven.) Pour marinade into drip pan under lamb and cook with indirect heat till medium rare, about 20 minutes per pound, or until internal temperature reaches 130 degrees. (You can toss some rosemary sprigs on the coals during the last few minutes of cooking to add flavor.)

Remove the leg and allow to sit while preparing gravy. Prepare a roux by combining **1/4 cup butter** and **1/4 cup flour** with **salt** and **pepper** in saucepan, and cook over medium heat till golden brown, stirring constantly. Add pan drippings and marinate slowly, stirring till well combined and slightly boiling. Adjust seasonings. Slice lamb and serve with gravy on the side.

Phil Allen

Phil Allen has been a television announcer and newscaster for 25 years. He recently left the NBC affiliate station in Phoenix to concentrate on his voiceover business. The 45-year-old veteran announcer is immediate past chairman of Scout-O-Rama, the biggest single fund-raiser for the Theodore Roosevelt Council of Boy Scouts of America. "*As an impoverished college student, unable to afford fine dining out, I found the only way I could afford to eat well was to cook well, so, my roommate and I watched Julia Child each Saturday morning and learned 'The Way to Cook'. We tried our efforts out on ladies we fancied and found the surest way to a woman's heart was to cook for her*". Phil is married to hospitality industry consultant Elin Jeffords.

DEEP DISH TACO PIE

2 C. Bisquick®
1/2 C. cold water
1 lb. hamburger, brown and drain
1 C. pepper, chopped
2 tomatoes, sliced thin
2 Tbsp. onion, minced
1 C. sour cream
2/3 C. mayonnaise
1 C. shredded cheese

Mix Bisquick and water. Spread into greased 9 x 13 pan, pushing sides up 1/2 inch. Spread meat into thin layer over Bisquick dough. Top with peppers and tomatoes. Mix onion, sour cream, mayonnaise and cheese together. Spread over meat mixture. Bake in 350 degree oven for 20 minutes. Serve with salsa.

Ronald Sandler

Ronald Sandler

Ronald Sandler is an orthopedic surgeon who has practiced in Mesa for the past 19 years. Dr. Sandler makes trips annually to do free surgery on the poor in foreign countries and particularly to Santarem, a poverty-stricken community on the Amazon River. Most of his patients are young children who are stricken with club feet. The doctor said there is a trememdous number of club-footed children in the Amazon basin, and he has not seen that many cases in one area in any other place he's ever been to. He has treated people in Bolivia, Peru, Ecuador, Honduras, Nicaragua, Mexico, St. Lucia, Pakistan and Taiwan. The former Peace Corps physician is currently the team physician for Red Mountain High School in Mesa and is the orthopaedic consultant for the Chicago Cubs baseball spring training camp. His honors include recipient of the Annual Luke Tupper Award; Esperanza; 1989 and recipient of Physician of the Year Award; Arizona Voluntary Medical Team; 1990.

MEXICAN MANICOTTI

8 manicotti shells
4 cooked chicken breasts, diced
1 C. low fat ricotta cheese
5 green onions, sliced
1/4 C. pitted black olives, chopped
1/4 C. red pepper, chopped
3 Tbsp. cilantro
1 sm. garlic clove, minced
1/2 tsp. Tabasco® sauce
1/2 C. Jack/pepper cheese, shredded
1 1/2 C. salsa (medium hot)
parsley for garnish

Preheat oven to 400 degrees. Grease 12 x 8 baking dish. Cook shells as label directs. Mix in large bowl cooked chicken, ricotta, onion, olives, pepper, cilantro, garlic and Tabasco sauce. Use a teaspoon to stuff shells with mixture. Place in baking dish. Top with cheese and salsa. Bake 20 minutes until hot and cheese is melted. Garnish with parsley and serve.

Yield: 4 servings.

Leah Wheatley Palmer

Leah Palmer is the executive director for Women Off Welfare (WOW!). Leah is an Idaho native converted to an Arizonian in 1986 by way of completing her Masters program in Communication Training and Development at Arizona State University. Her diversity of experience range from country girl rodeo queen to international model and travels to over 30 different countries. Her love for teaching, training and educating people about personal empowerment serves her well as the executive director for WOW! She said, *"The reward is watching peoples' lives change, becoming whole and healthy."*

CHICKEN-STUFFED PEPPERS

4 med. green peppers
1/3 C. onion, chopped
1 can (1 lb.) stewed tomatoes
2 C. cooked barley or rice
1/4 tsp. Tabasco® sauce
dash pepper
3 cooked chicken breasts, deboned and cubed
3/4 C. grated low-fat mozzarella or cheddar cheese

Cut tops of green peppers, remove seeds and membrane. Sauté onion in small amount of tomato liquid; add tomatoes, rice or barley, Tabasco, pepper, chicken and 1/2 of the cheese. Stand peppers upright in an 8-inch square baking dish; stuff with tomato-barley filling. Bake uncovered in 350 degree oven 25 to 30 minutes or until hot; sprinkle with remaining cheese. Return to oven until cheese melts.

Variation: In place of chicken, use 3/4 pound extra lean ground round, cooked and drained.

June Thomson

June Thomson

June Thomson is news anchor for KTSP-TV, Channel 10, in Phoenix. *"My short story concerns the culinary abilities of men and women, and how those talents change after marriage. Before meeting my husband, David, I knew nothing of the secrets to original or fanciful cooking. I was a reporter, and lived off fast-food fare and frozen chicken pot pies. David astounded me with his knowledge of marinade sauces and fixing a feast from scratch. He taught me everything he knew, and I, in turn, took great pride in becoming his cook. We got married and overnight David lost his magical skills in the kitchen. David now cannot boil an egg for Easter, and without me would starve. Instead of cooking from scratch, he scratches his head. I don't mind, because I love to cook and he doesn't mind doing the dishes—so it all works out in the end!!"*

CHICKEN BOMBAY

2 Tbsp. olive oil
8 chicken breasts, skinless, boneless
2 onions, sliced thin
2 bell peppers, 1 red, 1 green, chopped coarse
1 Tbsp. chopped garlic
3 Tbsp. curry powder
1 can (14 1/2 oz.) whole tomatoes
4 Tbsp. dried currants (or cranberries)
1 tsp. thyme
1 tsp. pepper
2 tsp. salt
2 Tbsp. chopped parsley
2 C. white wine

In large skillet, sauté chicken in olive oil until lightly browned. Remove chicken and set aside. Add onions and cook until soft. Add bell peppers, garlic, curry powder, tomatoes, currants, thyme, salt, pepper, parsley and white wine. Stir well. Return chicken to skillet and simmer covered approximately 1 to 1 1/2 hours.

Preston Westmoreland

Preston Westmoreland

Preston Westmoreland is the host of KTAR's *The Preston Westmoreland Show* and is KTAR's first daytime talk-show host and longest-running personality. For over 14 years he has been at the microphone interviewing over 19,000 guests and airing the show from San Diego to the nation's capitol, from hot-air balloons to political conventions, even inside the Arizona State Prison. Preston has won more than twenty broadcasting awards, and is a member of the team that won journalism's highest honor, the Peabody Award, in 1988 for coverage of the impeachment of Arizona governor Evan Mecham. In addition to his radio career, Preston is an avid pilot and he and his wife of 20 years, Nancy, are big fans of flying their Piper Saratoga into remote areas and camping. In July of 1992, Preston hosted, photographed and produced the first video on desert survival, called *Stay Alive*.

PASTA CLAUDIO

1/2 med. yellow onion	1 can (14 oz.) crushed
3 cloves garlic	tomatoes
1/4 C. olive oil (extra virgin)	2 or 3 anchovies or equiva-
1 sprig fresh basil	lent anchovy paste
1 sprig fresh oregano	1 pkg. (16 oz.) (semolina
3 Tbsp. salt	wheat) spaghetti

Mince onion and cut garlic cloves in half or thirds. In large skillet, gently sauté onion and garlic in olive oil over low heat, stirring often until onion is transparent. Do not brown. Add anchovies and mix with wooden spoon until anchovy is dissolved. Add tomatoes, 5-6 basil leaves and 5-6 oregano leaves. Stir gently, reduce to simmer and stir occasionally.

Bring 3 quarts water to a boil. Add salt and spaghetti. Test spaghetti at 8 minutes and every 30 seconds thereafter until spaghetti is cooked, but still slightly firm in the middle. Lift spaghetti from still-boiling water directly into the skillet of sauce, allowing some of the salted water to drip into the sauce. Increase heat under skillet and gently roll the spaghetti with 2 large slotted spoons in the sauce for approximately 1 minute. This finishes the cooking of the spaghetti and absorbs some of the sauce into the pasta.

Serve in bowls and top with a few leaves of oregano, basil and fresh grated parmesan. Add a basket of crusty hot bread and at least 1 bottle of good Italian wine. A green salad wouldn't hurt, either!

Jerry Scott

Jerry Scott

"This recipe was given to me by our friends, Claudio and Annemarie of Verona, Italy. It was the first meal cooked in our new home in Cave Creek (and if the stove had been adjusted properly, I would still have eyebrows!)" Jerry Scott has been writing and drawing the syndicated comic strip *"Nancy"* for the last 10 years and writes the syndicated comic strip *"Baby Blues"* (drawn by his partner, Rick Kirkman). He lives in Cave Creek, AZ with his wife of 18 years, Kim.

COTTAGE CHEESE RAISIN CASSEROLE

1/2 lb. noodles—spaghetti
    or macaroni or both
box of raisins to taste

2 C. cottage or pot cheese
4 Tbsp. butter

Cook and drain noodles. Add butter. Stir and add raisins and cottage cheese.

Kathy Shocket

Kathy Shocket

Kathy Shocket is a reporter for KTSP-TV, Channel 10, in Phoenix and is a columnist for *The Arizona Republic*. Kathy added a personal note: *"I prefer recipes that require as little preparation as possible. Because I have little time to cook (and wash dishes) these days, I'm better at making reservations."*

B-B-Q BEEF
(The Easiest Recipe in the World)

3 to 4 lbs. boneless chuck or rump roast
1 - 32 oz. bottle Bill Johnson's® BBQ Sauce (or your favorite)

Cover roast with sauce and cook on high in crockpot 6 to 8 hours. When meat begins to fall apart, remove from pot and shred with 2 forks. Stir meat back into sauce. Stir and serve on rolls or on baked potatoes.

Larry Burleson

Larry Burleson

Larry Burleson of Mesa found out he was named one of nine unsung heroes in American industry by seeing his picture in Industry Week magazine. Apparently Larry was on vacation when everyone else learned of the awards announcement. Larry, is the manager of Supply Management for Motorola's Government Electronics Group in Scottsdale. Larry shared this note, *"My wife cooks for us and caters as a business—so I don't cook, but even I can make this."*

AGNOLOTTI

1 pkg. won ton wraps (60 per package. Unused wrappers
    can be frozen for use at a later time.)
Filling, (recipe follows)
Tomato Cumin Vinaigrette, (recipe follows)
parmesan cheese for grating

FILLING

6 green onions, trimmed	1 tsp. chili powder
1/3 C. cilantro leaves	1/4 tsp. powdered cumin
8 oz. cream cheese	pinch of salt
1/2 C. sour cream	

Finely chop green onions and cilantro leaves, or use food
processor. In a medium-sized bowl, blend together cream cheese,
sour cream, chili powder, and cumin. Stir in the finely chopped green
onion and cilantro. Add pinch of salt if desired.

Yield: about 4 dozen half-moon-shaped filled pasta.

Tomato Cumin Vinaigrette

4 tsp. lemon juice	8 green onions, chopped
2 Tbsp. vinegar	2 clove garlic, minced
1/2 tsp. cumin	2 Tbsp. cilantro,
pinch of salt	finely chopped
1/2 C. canned tomato sauce	2 C. diced Roma tomatoes
1/2 C. vegetable oil	(4 to 5 med. sized)

In a medium-sized bowl, whisk together the lemon juice, vinegar,
cumin, salt and tomato sauce. While whisking, slowly drizzle in the
oil. Stir in the green onion, garlic, cilantro and tomatoes. Cover and
refrigerate for at least 30 minutes. Can be prepared the night before.
Yield: About 2 1/2 cups

To assemble: Place filling in a pastry bag with tip and squeeze
out about 1 teaspoonful of filling onto the center of each won ton
wrapper (or spoon filling onto wrappers). Moisten edges with
cornstarch/water mixture (1 teaspoon per 1/2 cup water) and fold
corner to corner (to form a triangle), press edges to seal. Using a
cookie or biscuit cutter, cut out half-moon shapes and place on dish
towel. Repeat procedure to make desired amount. Cook agnolotti

in boiling water for approximately 3 to 4 minutes or until al dente. Spoon Tomato Cumin Vinaigrette over the cooked, stuffed pasta and top with freshly grated parmesan cheese.

Richard S. Vonier

Richard S. Vonier

Dick Vonier is the editor of *Phoenix Magazine*. *"When the gifts were doled out, cooking skills were not among those I received, You're hearing from a man who once wrote a column entitled, 'The Better Cheddars Diet'. So when invited to provide a recipe for this cookbook, I did what any sensible editor would do: I got together with Phoenix Magazine's culinary expert and food critic Donald Downes and we decided to provide this offering, an original by Donald, on behalf of the publication. My background is in writing and editing, and eating lunch at my desk."*

Mr. Vonier has worked for publications in Milwaukee and Chicago and was formerly assistant managing editor of the *Tucson Citizen* (Tucson's afternoon daily newspaper), was involved in the start-up of *Arizona Trend* magazine (a valley-based business magazine), and was publisher of *City Magazine* in Tucson. He joined *Phoenix Magazine* in May 1989, six months before it was purchased by Media America Corporation.

Donald Downes

Donald Downes is a graduate of Scottsdale Culinary Institute and won first prize in their Festival's First Annual Student Scholarship Competition. He then put his classroom knowledge to work as a cook at the internationally renowned Boulders Resort, in Carefree, for three seasons. During that time, he taught cooking classes at Two Plates Full (a Scottsdale kitchen and gourmet ware store) as well as writing a column in the *Scottsdale Progress*. Presently, he divides his time between Phoenix Magazine and his freelance food writing/food consulting business.

MONTEZUMA CHICKEN

6 C. cooked, boned, skinned, shredded chicken
1 pt. sour cream
1 dozen corn tortillas in 1 1/2" pieces
1/2 lb. Jack cheese, shredded

GREEN SAUCE
1 can (14 oz.) tomatillos
1 sm. onion, cut up
2 cloves garlic
1 can (4 oz.) diced green chiles
1/2 Tbsp. cilantro
1 tsp. salt
1/2 tsp. sugar

Whirl until smooth in blender.

In greased 9 X 12 pan layer:

1/2 chicken	**1/2 tortillas**
1/2 green sauce	**1/2 cheese**
1/2 sour cream	**and, repeat.**

Cover with foil and bake at 375 degrees for 45 minutes. Uncover and cook until bubbling. Serve with one of the following toppings: green onions, sour cream, salsa. Serve with bread, tossed salad, and flan.

Dan Duncan

Dan Duncan is president and chief executive officer of Mesa United Way. Dan is a community activist who is driven by a strong need to make his community better. He provides vision and enthusiasm to promote volunteerism in Mesa.

GREEN CHILE GRITS CASSEROLE

1 lb. browned sausage
1 1/2 C. grits cooked by directions (instant)

Combine with cooked grits:

3 beaten eggs
1 stick margarine
8 oz. green chile
3 C. grated cheddar longhorn cheese

Spread 1/2 grits mixture into 12 x 8 dish. Cover with cooked sausage and then rest of grits. Bake in 350 degree oven for 1 hour. Top with more cheese.

Janet Napolitano

Janet Napolitano is a partner at the law firm of Lewis and Roca in Phoenix and was one of the attorneys representing Anita Hill in the Clarence Thomas supreme court hearings. She chairs the State Bar Committee on Civil Procedure, and belongs to numerous legal honoraries including the American Law Institute, to which she was elected in 1989. She is the youngest lawyer, in terms of years of practice, ever to receive the coveted "AV" rating from Martindale-Hubbell, a national legal rating service. Janet is the U.S. attorney-designate for the District of Arizona. She received her undergraduate degree from the University of Santa Clara and currently is a member of the University's Board of Regents. She received her law degree from the University of Virginia School of Law. She resides in Phoenix.

PORK CHOPS & RHUBARB

6 pork chops	3 Tbsp. flour
4 slices bread crumbs	pepper
3/4 C. brown sugar	salt
1/2 tsp. cinnamon	rosemary
1/4 tsp. allspice	
2 1/4 lb. rhubarb cut into 1 1/2-inch squares	

Brown chops in skillet sprayed with **non-stick vegetable spray** and **1 tablespoon oil.** Save drippings. Mix all ingredients except chops. Layer rhubarb mixture, chops, rhubarb mix, etc. in 13 x 8 pan. Bake in 350 degree oven for 1 hour—45 minutes covered, 15 minutes uncovered.

Dolli Peralta

E.J. "Dolli" Peralta

Dolli Peralta is the executive director of Make-A-Wish-Foundation in Phoenix serving Central and Southern Arizona.

Do You Believe in Fairy Godmothers?

Most seventeen year old high school students don't believe in Fairy Godmothers. Although my friends may think I'm crazy, I happen to regard these illusionary wish granters as quite real. My reason for believing the way I do is that on March 5, 1991, I was visited by three of them bearing strange gifts. They said they were from the Make-A-Wish Foundation and asked me what my wish was. I told them that I wanted to go on the Big Red Boat Vacation. This once-in-a-lifetime trip includes admission to the Disney Magic Kingdom, Epcot Center, M.G.M. Studios, Kennedy Space Center and a cruise to the Bahamas.

One month after their visit, one of the Fairy Godmothers called me and said that my wish would come true. As you can see, anyone who has a wish granted like I did would end up believing in Fairy Godmothers too!

Greg

THE MARSH CHICKEN CHALUPA

1 onion, diced
4 Tbsp. butter
1 can cream of chicken soup
1 can cream of mushroom soup
2/3 C. milk
1 can green chile
12 corn tortillas, cut into strips
8 boneless chicken breasts, cooked and cubed
1 lb. sharp cheddar cheese, grated

Sauté onion and 4 tablespoons butter. Add soups, milk, green chili and heat to medium. Grease 9 x 13 casserole dish with butter. On bottom of casserole, put 1/2 tortillas, 1/2 chicken and cheese and pour in half the soup. Repeat (layer). Top with cheese. Cover and refrigerate 24 hours. Cook in 300 degree oven for 1 1/2 hours.

James E. Marsh

Jim Marsh is the former director of the Arizona Department of Commerce and served as the governor's executive assistant for economic and business development. He attended the University of Arizona where he studied business administration and psychology. He holds a seat on the executive council of the Arizona Economic Council and is a member of the advisory board for the Biltmore Bank. He is a member of the Phoenix Thunderbirds, promoting sports in the metropolitan area, and a member of the Church of Saint Maria Goretti. Marsh boasts a two-handicap golf game, which comes in handy when entertaining prospective clients on the golf course.

LINGUINE TRICOLORI

"This dish has inspired many a performance!"

8 sun-dried tomatoes
1/3 lb. linguine, cooked al dente
5 to 7 Tbsp. olive oil
5 to 7 lg. cloves of garlic, pressed
1/2 C. carrot sticks, cut in 1-inch pieces
Italian seasonings
3/4 C. bite-sized broccoli buds
black pepper
freshly grated Parmesan

Preparation: rehydrate tomatoes in small bowl, slightly covered with water. This is best done by: 1) microwave for 2 minutes —20 minutes before eating, or 2) soak at room temperature for 1 to 2 hours. Set tomatoes aside, in their deep red juice.

While pasta is cooking, heat olive oil in large pan at low medium temperature. With 4 minutes to go before pasta is done, add pressed garlic. As soon as garlic turns white (45 seconds to 1 minute), add carrots and Italian seasoning. Stir together for another minute. Add broccoli and black pepper. Stir.

By now, pasta is ready to be strained. Pour strained pasta together with sun-dried tomatoes and their deep red juice into pan and stir together with garlic, olive oil, etc. The pasta will take on the rich flavor of the sun-dried tomatoes and the rest. As soon as it is mixed, put pasta on plate and toss with Parmesan. Pour vegetables and juices over pasta and top with a little more freshly grated parmesan.

Bon appetit!
Yield: 2 servings.

Eric Black

Eric Black is the music director of the Mesa Symphony.

AUNT BOO'S MEATLOAF

"This recipe comes from Sam's sister, Beth, known to all of us as 'Aunt Boo.' Aunt Boo is a chef in Philadelphia. Her recipes are favorites with our three children—anything from Aunt Boo has got to be good. Is it her name or the food? Who knows, but if the kids eat it, it's great by me."

1 1/2 lb. - 2 lb. ground turkey
1 1/2 tsp. sesame oil
3 cloves garlic, minced
1/4 C. oatmeal
1/2 C. bread crumbs
2 Tbsp. soy sauce
2 Tbsp. sherry
salt and pepper to taste
1 sm. onion
celery and carrots cut in 3-inch lengths

Combine turkey, sesame oil, minced garlic, oatmeal, bread crumbs, soy sauce and sherry by hand. Add salt and pepper. Shape into loaf in medium size covered baking pan. Surround with onion, celery and carrots. Bake covered in 375 degree oven for 1 hour. Add 1/2 cup chicken broth after 45 minutes.

Sam Coppersmith

Sam Coppersmith

Sam Coppersmith represents District 1 in the United States House of Representatives. Coppersmith is a member of the Public Works and Transportation Committee and the Science, Space and Technology Committee. Before he was elected in November of 1992, he practiced business and real estate law in Phoenix. He has been president and director of Planned Parenthood of Central and Northern Arizona, was a member and chair of the Phoenix Board of Adjustment, and a member of the 1988 Phoenix Citizens Bond Committee and Phoenix Surface Transportation Advisory Committee.

5 STAR, 5 STEP, 5 MINUTE, HIGH FIBER VITA MEAL

1/4 C. water
I lg. apple or pear peeled, cored and sliced
4 oz. Esseje bread (available in health food stores)
1 Tbsp. brewers yeast
2 Tbsp. real maple syrup
1 Tbsp. lemon juice

1. Simmer the 1/4 cup of water.
2. Put pear or apple in water and simmer for 2 minutes covered.
3. Add bread broken into 1" chunks and simmer for 1 minute.
4. Remove from heat and let sit covered for 2 minutes.
5. Stir in brewers yeast, maple syrup, and lemon juice.

Lorene Yarnell

Lorene Yarnell

Lorene Yarnell is the pantomime artist and partner in the Shields and Yarnell team. Lorene now resides in Sedona and started a school of dance there. She and Robert Shields, are teaming up again in a United States tour. See Robert's "Mirliton De Paris" recipe (page199).

SPAGHETTI CARBONARA

1/4 lb. prosciutto (sliced thinly and cut in strips)
1/4 lb. pancetta (available in Italian
    groceries or substitute bacon)
1 yellow onion, minced
1/2 lb. No. 8 spaghetti
1/4 lb. butter
2 eggs
1/4 C. fresh grated Romano cheese
1/4 C. fresh grated Parmesan cheese

Sauté proscuitto and pancetta, which should both be cut in small strips, in medium frying pan. After fat has been rendered add onion and sauté until golden brown. Meanwhile put spaghetti into a sufficient amount of rapidly boiling water and cook until al dente (firm but cooked). Place spaghetti in colander to drain, keeping cooking pot handy. After sufficient draining return spaghetti to pot and add butter, eggs and cheese, stirring vigorously until well blended. Top with meat and onion mixture, stirring slightly. Immediately place onto serving plates, passing additional grated cheeses as desired.

Yield: Serves 2 healthy or 3 normal appetites.

Jim Ahearn

Jim's official title is Special Agent In Charge of the Arizona Federal Bureau of Investigation for the U. S. Department of Justice. In other words, Jim is the head FBI guy in Arizona. Rumor has it that Jim is a very good cook and would enjoy being a food critic!

JEWISH HAMBURGERS

2 lbs. of ground lean chuck
1 sm. grated onion
4 eggs
4 slices white bread without crust, soaked in water
2 cloves minced garlic
1/2 tsp. pepper
1/2 tsp. salt

Mix all above ingredients in bowl and make 8 to 10 patties which should be rolled in **Matzo Meal**.

Slice **2 large onions** and **4 peeled Russet potatoes**. Season potatoes with **salt, pepper,** and **paprika**. Sauté onions and potatoes in about **4 tablespoons of hot oil** until golden brown, then add hamburger patties until done.

Harlan Capin

Harlin Capin is the president and chief executive officer of Capin Mercantile Corporation in Nogales, Arizona. His company operates 31 Factory 2-U discount stores. Owned by 15 family members, tradition is their commitment, which keeps the factory in Nogales. Capin is the largest private employer in Santa Cruz County.

DAVID'S FAVORITE FETTUCCINE

1 recipe homemade noodle
    dough cut medium or wide
boiling salted water
1 to 1 1/2 C. soft butter

2 C. Parmesan cheese
3/4 C. heavy cream
freshly ground black
    pepper

Cook noodles in a large quantity of boiling, salted water until tender. Allow about four minutes for thin noodles, longer for thick ones. Drain well.

Place noodles in hot casserole over low heat. Add butter, grated cheese and cream (must be heavy), a little at a time, tossing gently after each addition. Season with freshly ground black pepper to taste.

J. David Hann

David Hann is the mayor of the town of Paradise Valley.

FULL OF BEANS

1 - 14 oz. can of pork and beans
2 - 6 oz. cans lima beans
1 - 12 oz. can kidney beans
6 slices of bacon
1 onion

3/4 cups brown sugar
1 small brick of mild
    cheese chunks
1 Tbsp. Worcestershire
    sauce

Drain lima and kidney beans and dump into a bowl with pork and beans. Fry six slices of bacon, cut into small pieces and add to beans. Add sliced onion to bacon grease and cook. Drain off grease. Add to beans. Mix in the next three ingredients thoroughly, sprinkle with **Parmesan cheese** and bake at 350 degreees for 30 to 40 minutes.

Note: Any combination of your favorite beans can be used.

Robert Chandler

Robert Chandler is the superintendent of the Grand Canyon National Park.

CUBAN BLACK BEANS

1 bag black beans
1 1/2 lg. onions
1 bell pepper
4 cloves garlic or,
   1 tsp. garlic powder
1/4 C. olive oil
4 tsp. salt

1 tsp. black pepper
1/4 tsp. oregano powder
3 bay leaves
2 Tbsp. sugar
2 Tbsp. vinegar
2 Tbsp. sherry or any
   white wine

Clean and rinse beans. Soak in about 10 cups water overnight. Cook beans in same water until almost tender (about 1 hour). Add more water if necessary.

Cut onion, bell pepper and garlic into small pieces. Place in blender with small amount of water and puree until smooth. Add to beans.

Add the rest of the ingredients except the vinegar and wine and simmer until thick. Add vinegar and wine and simmer 1/2 hour longer. Remove bay leaves and stir well before serving. Serve over rice.

Yield: 6 to 10 servings.

Michael A. Laosa

Mike Laosa is the publisher and president of Cox Arizona Publications, Inc. Cox Arizona Publications includes the *Mesa Tribune*, the *Gilbert Tribune*, the *Tempe Daily News Tribune*, the *Chandler Arizona Tribune*, the *Scottsdale Progress Tribune*, the *Arizona Pennysaver, Clipper magazine* and *Cox Infolink*. A native of Cuba, Mike grew up in Austin, Texas, where he began his newspaper career with the *Austin American-Statesman*. He knows his Cuban food.

BLACK BEANS

1 lb. black beans (soak overnight and drain excess liquid)
6 C. water (you may prefer chicken broth)
2 - 15 oz. cans tomato sauce
1 carrot, grated
1 onion, finely chopped
2 or 3 cloves garlic, chopped
1 tsp. red pepper (cayenne) crushed
2 to 3 squares Bakers® unsweetened chocolate
1/2 tsp. chili powder
8 whole pepper corns
1 tsp. olive oil (optional)
1 tsp. oregano
salt to taste

In a large sauce pan, bring the above ingredients to a boil. Reduce heat and simmer all day. Stir occasionally and add liquid if necessary. This recipe works well with a crock pot, too.

Anne Coe

Anne Coe

Anne Coe is a 4th generation native of Arizona. She is a two-dimensional artist who paints subjects around the world and particularly the west. Her art depicts her feelings as a preservationist and conservationist concerned about the changeover problems and challenges from the days of the old west to the days of modernization of today. Anne's art is exhibited at the Elaine Horwitz Gallery.

RATATOUILLE AMERICAN STYLE

1/4 C. vegetable oil	1 tsp. marjoram
2 cloves garlic, crushed	1/2 tsp. oregano
1 med. onion, chopped	dash of ground rosemary
1 med. bell pepper, cubed	3 carrots, sliced
1 leek, sliced	1 med. or 2 sm. zucchini
1 sm. eggplant, cubed	and/or yellow squash,
3 Tbsp. dry red wine	sliced
28 oz. can stewed tomatoes	salt and pepper to taste
1 bay leaf	2 Tbsp. tomato paste
1 tsp. basil	Parmesan cheese, grated

Heat the vegetable oil in a large heavy pot. Sauté garlic, onion, peppers and leek over medium heat until onion begins to turn transparent. Add eggplant, wine and stewed tomatoes. Add herbs. Stir, cover and simmer over low heat until eggplant is tender enough to be pricked with a fork (10-15 minutes). Meanwhile, steam the carrots until tender. Do not overcook. Add zucchini and carrots to eggplant mixture. Cover and simmer 10 minutes. Add salt, pepper and tomato paste. Mix well. Continue to simmer until vegetables reach desired tenderness. Top with grated Parmesan cheese. Serve with rice or French bread.

Yield: Serves 4 to 6.

Amy A. Douglass

Amy A. Douglass is the museum administrator for the Tempe Historical Museum.

COLOMBIAN POTATOES WITH CHEESE
(Papas Chorreadas)

8 - 12 sm. red skinned new potatoes
2 Tbsp. butter
1 med. onion, finely chopped
4 lg. green onions, cut in 1 inch lengths
2 lg. tomatoes, peeled and chopped
1/2 C. whipping cream
1 Tbsp. finely chopped fresh cilantro
1/2 tsp. oregano leaves
1/4 tsp. ground cumin
salt and pepper
1 C. shredded mozzarella cheese

Scrub potatoes, do not peel. Place potatoes in large pan, cover with water and boil, covered, until tender when pierced, about 20 minutes. Drain and place in serving dish, keep warm. In frying pan, melt butter over medium heat, add chopped onion and green onion and cook until limp. Add tomatoes and cook, stirring often for 5 minutes. Stir in cream, cilantro, oregano, cumin, salt and pepper to taste. While stirring, slowly add the cheese and cook until cheese is melted. Spoon over potatoes and serve at once.

Yield: Serves 4 to 6.

Pam Castano

Pam Castano

Pam Castano is known from San Francisco to New York as an artist who creates environmental art work. Kites, banners, clocks, and ribbon clusters made of nylon, steel tubing, perforated metal, vinyl fabric, neon, and powder coated aluminum are a few of her claims to fame. She has designs at businesses, hospitals, airports, malls, and universities throughout the country. Her art adds life and spontaneity to such places as American Express, Arizona Public Service, DeVry Institute, Dick Fritsche Architects, St. Joseph's Hospital, St. Luke's Hospital, University of Arizona, Arizona State University, and Mesa's Superstition Springs Center.

D'AMICO'S BROCCOLI & SHELLS

2 lbs. broccoli
1 lb. med. or lg. pasta shells
2 C. chicken broth
5 to 7 cloves of fresh garlic

1/4 C. olive oil (extra virgin)
4 Tbsp. butter
1 fresh tomato

Bring a pot of water to boil and add **one tsp. salt**. Add broccoli cut into flowerettes. Cook on medium heat. When broccoli turns bright green and is slightly tender, scoop out broccoli with strainer, keep the water. Add pasta shells to the water and cook on medium heat. When pasta is al dente, slightly tender, strain and splash with cold tap water.

Combine chicken broth, minced garlic, olive oil, butter, diced tomato and broccoli in a large frying pan. Bring to boil. Add pasta and toss together. Pour into large pasta dish and sprinkle on **Peccorino Romano cheese**. Serve immediately. (Sometimes I add garlic powder to broth and butter to add extra flavor. The Peccorino Romano cheese makes a big difference to the flavor but is very salty.

Yield: Serves 4 to 6.

Rick D'Amico

Rick D'Amico

Rick D'Amico is news anchor for KTSP-TV, Channel 10 News, in Phoenix.

BABA GHANOUJ

2 lg. round eggplants
2 cloves garlic
1 med. size lemon
1/2 C. tahini *
1/2 C. olive oil
fresh spearmint leaves (optional)
l pomegranate (optional)

Peel off leaves from eggplants, leave hard stem on for later handling. Poke eggplants with a skewer or knife for even cooking. Wrap each eggplant with one layer of aluminum foil. Bake on grill until soft, approximately 35 minutes on medium heat. Remove foil, hold eggplant with fork through stem and peel off skin, do it under cold water if too hot. Place in mixing bowl and beat using wooden mortar until consistent, can be stringy. (I don't suggest using blender, but is commonly done.)

Smash garlic in small bowl, squeeze lemon over garlic and mix well with eggplants. Add the tahini, also add salt and pepper to taste and mix well. The tahini will change the color of the mixture to a creamy color.

Place on a plate. Position mint leaves on the edges of the plate, add a tablespoon of the pomegranate berries, spread olive oil on surface and serve. Add more lemon and salt to taste. Eat with warm pita bread as a dip. Tastes good with a leafy salad and with tomatoes.

*Tahini is a roasted sesame seed paste that can be found in Middle Eastern Stores or from some health food stores and is a main ingredient in many Arabic dishes.

Selim Hammoud

Selim Hammoud is a Northern Arizona University graduate and engineer working with Failure Analysis Associates, Inc. Selim was born in Lebanon and came to Arizona in 1979. He is very active in the Arab American community in the Valley both for political and cultural events, and is very knowledgeable about the Islamic culture.

CHOPPED LIVER RECIPE

1 lb. chicken livers
1/4 lb. butter (+ 1 Tbsp. chicken fat)
2 sliced onions
3 hard boiled eggs
1 chopped sweet onion (to add at end)
salt and pepper
mayonnaise

Boil livers (just covered) in salted water until pink (4 to 5 minutes). Heat butter and chicken fat and sauté sliced onions. Chop eggs with sautéed onions. Chop livers coarsely. Add small amount of mayonnaise, mix together, and season to taste.

Marion Herrman

Marion Herrman

Marion Herrman is a Sedona commercial artist and was a wartime volunteer performer for the USO (United Service Organizations) during the late '40s until 1950. As a homemaker and mother, she also participated in numerous volunteer and civic activities. She was a professional pop/jazz/swing singer in New York City area, working with major studio and jazz musicians for clubs, television, and private functions. During the '70s, she owned, managed, and performed with Mitchell Ayres' Big Band in major nightclubs, and also with the highly successful Supper Club "*Tuxedo Junction*". In 1980, she and her husband received United Fund's Humanitarian Award. She is involved in many of Sedona's cultural and community activities and as a professional sculptor exhibits "JazzArt" bronzes at the Ratliff Williams Gallery. She is presently accumulating detailed information on performing arts facilities all over the country.

CHILE CHEESE SOUFFLÉ

8 oz. Kraft® Light Natural Jack
with Pepper Cheese
8 oz. Kraft® Cracker Barrel Light Sharp Cheddar
1 can whole green chiles, washed and seeds removed
4 egg whites
4 oz. skim evaporated milk
1 jar (small size) Pace® Picante Sauce, mild or medium (I'm
not brave enough for hot)

Preheat oven to 350 degrees. Grate cheese by hand or better yet, food processor. Mix both cheeses together in bowl. Spray bottom of square glass pan with Pam® and split chiles and line bottom of pan with them—it's a stretch, if you are a real chile fan use 2 cans for bottom. Gently dump the cheese in pan and fluff it up to allow for air space.

Whip the egg whites in small bowl until stiff and fold in the evaporated milk. Pour mixture evenly over cheese and chiles. Spread it around with knife and bake in oven for 40 minutes. Set the buzzer and when it goes off pour the jar of picante sauce on the top and bake for another 20 minutes.

This is a great pot luck recipe. Also "nukes" well as a left-over. You can make ahead the night before if you cook 50 minutes and refrigerate. The next morning add the picante and heat for 20 to 30 minutes at 350 degrees or microwave for several minutes.

Yield: Serves 8.

Peggy Rubach

Peggy Rubach

Peggy Rubach is the former mayor of the city of Mesa. She is currently the Special Assistant at the Arizona Department of Transportation. She said she used to make this recipe the high caloric, fat and cholesterol way, but is trying to become more nutrition-conscious. She modified it by reducing it 100 calories per serving by lowering the fat and raising the protein.

ARIZONA BAKED BEANS

1 med. onion, chopped
1 tsp. butter
1 - 16 oz. can red kidney beans
1 - 16 oz. can B & M® baked beans
1 C. ketchup

1 C. packed brown sugar
1 tsp. vinegar
1 tsp. yellow French's® mustard
4 strips fried bacon, cooled and crumbled

In a skillet, sauté chopped onion with butter. In a large baking pot, combine kidney beans, B & M baked beans, ketchup, brown sugar, vinegar, mustard, and crumbled bacon. Combine and stir, adding sautéed onions. Mix well. Bake in covered dish at 350 - 375 degrees for 35 minutes or until piping hot. This dish is perfect for a barbecue. Enjoy!

John McCain

John McCain

John McCain represents Arizona in the United States Senate. After a distinguished military career and two terms as a U. S. Representative, McCain was re-elected to a second term as senator in 1992. He serves on the Committee on Armed Services; the Committee on Commerce, Science, and Transportation; the Select Committee on Indian Affairs; the Special Committee on Aging and the Committee on Governmental Affairs. Senator McCain is the Chairman of the International Republican Institute and serves as Chairman of the Energy and Environment Study Conference. He graduated from the U. S. Naval Academy, and was a prisoner of war in Vietnam for five and a half years.

SHARON'S SCALLOPED CARROTS

4 C. sliced or diced carrots
1 med. onion, chopped
3 Tbsp. butter
dash pepper
1 can cream of celery soup
1/2 tsp. salt
1/2 C. diced cheese (your choice)
   TOPPING
3 C. herb flavored croutons
1/2 C. melted butter

Cook carrots in salted water until almost done. Sauté onions in butter. Combine carrots, onions, soup, salt and pepper. Put in baking dish and bake at 350 degrees until heated. Put on topping and bake until brown. Dancingly Delicious!

Sharon Meko

Sharon Meko is the artistic director of the Ballet Etudes. Since 1979, Sharon has pursued her love of ballet in Arizona where she danced with the Mesa Civic Ballet (presently Ballet Arizona), and has choreographed for the Arizona Metropolitan Ballet Junior Co., and served as a guest teacher. She was on the faculty of the Dance Department at Arizona State University, and has taught for Profile for Dance. A teacher of ballet for 19 years, Sharon is presently director of ballet at Jeanne Wright Dance Academy. She was honored by the Mesa Chamber of Commerce and Arts when she was named "The Artist of the Year" in 1991.

SKATER'S SPECIAL POTATOES

3 lg. baking potatoes
1/2 onion (optional)
1/4 C. cooking oil
Lawry's® Season Salt
pepper

2 Tbsp. butter or margarine
cheese (normally mozzarella
or cheddar, but feel free
to be different!)
bacon bits

Slice potatoes (and onion if you want to be a little bit different) into 1/8 inch or thinner slices and place in hot oil in skillet. Oil should be just a thin layer and not cover the potatoes. Turn the potatoes at short intervals. After a few minutes add a generous amount of season salt and pepper. Add the butter and continue turning. Continue turning until the potatoes are cooked. Lay out paper towels and drain the potatoes. Place more paper towels on top to soak up as much oil as possible.

The next step can either be done on a plate in the microwave or in the oven. Once the potatoes have been drained place slices of cheese on top of and within the pile of spuds, cover with a generous amount of bacon bits, and cook until the cheese is melted.

Hal Marron

Hal Marron is a 37-year-young engineer who started skating in Southern California at about age 10. His family moved to Arizona in 1972 when he was 16 and he graduated from Arcadia High School. He spent two years at Arizona State University and then transferred to the University of California at Irvine receiving his degree in 1979. He qualified for the U.S. Figure Skating Championships for the first time in 1975. He qualified in three separate events. After that, he decided to limit himself to pairs and ice dancing. He and his sister placed 5th at the 1980 Championships and were named as alternates to the Olympic team. They represented the U.S. at a competition in Japan in 1980 and then retired after the 1981 U. S. Championships. He currently judges U. S. Championships and was at America West Arena in Phoenix this year doing just that!

KUGELIS
(Potato Pudding)

10 lg. potatoes
1 med. onion
5 slices bacon
1/2 C. hot milk or
    evaporated milk

2 tsp. salt
1/4 tsp. pepper
3 eggs

Peel and fine grate the potatoes and onion. Cut bacon into narrow pieces and fry until crisp. Pour fat and bacon over the potatoes. Add hot milk. Add beaten eggs, salt and pepper. Bake in 400 degree oven for 15 minutes. Reduce heat to 375 degrees, bake 45 minutes longer. Cut into squares. Serve hot with sour cream. Use as a main course or side dish.

Suggestions on making good Kugelis:

1. Start with old potatoes

2. The grated potato mixture should be about 2 to 2 1/2 inches deep in the baking dish.

3. Use a high temperature at the start of baking, then finish cooking at the lower temperature.

There are many different versions. Each recipe is individualized in texture and flavor by adding farina, oatmeal, or bread crumbs to the basic grated mixture.

Joan A. Newth

Joan A. Newth

Joan Newth is Mesa's 1993 Woman of the Year. Though Joan's accomplishments and endeavors have been many, the one that has a special place in her heart is The Red Ribbon Campaign which she started several years ago. "*Lithuanian cuisine reflects the good, solid, thrifty people with a long agricultural background. Typical native food is hearty, nourishing and not highly seasoned. Without a doubt, the one recipe among all Lithuanians that stimulates the nostalgic nerve, and revives memories of the fragrant aromas of mothers cooking is 'Kugelis' or Potato Pudding.*"

HARRY'S HASH

1/4 C. olive oil
8 lg. potatoes (cut into
    1" cubes)
4 med. onions, sliced
    vertically

    Preheat oven to 400 degrees. Place oil in shallow baking pan and add all ingredients. Mix well. Bake uncovered for 1 1/2 hours, turning potatoes over about every 10 minutes. Preparation is about 30 minutes. Super with steak, hamburgers, and breaded fish.

    Yield: Serves 6.

Harry E. Mitchell

Harry E. Mitchell

    Harry Mitchell is the mayor of the city of Tempe.

POTATO CHEESE CASSEROLE

1- 32 oz. bag frozen hash browns	1 can cream of chicken soup
1 pt. sour cream	1 stick margarine
1/2 tsp. salt	2 C. Velveeta® cheese

Heat sour cream, salt, chicken soup, margarine, and cheese in saucepan. Place hash browns in casserole dish and cover with heated ingredients. Cover the dish and bake in oven at 325 degrees for 30 minutes.

Howie Wennes

Howie E. Wennes

Howie Wennes is the Bishop for Evangelical Lutheran Church in America, Arizona-Southern Nevada Synod, "The Grand Canyon Synod".

CORN CASSEROLE

2 cans creamed corn	1/2 tsp. baking powder
1/4 C. corn meal	1/3 C. Wesson® Oil
3/4 tsp. garlic salt	2 eggs

Mix all ingredients and layer with **1 can Ortega long green chiles** and **1/2 C. grated sharp cheddar cheese**. Top with **1/4 C. grated cheese**. Bake in 450 degree oven for 45 minutes.

Pat Wright

Patricia "Pat" Wright

Pat Wright of Glendale is an Arizona state senator representing District 17. The 41st Legislature (1993-1994) Directory lists her occupation as homemaker/legislator. Committee assignments are: Finance, Chair; Transportation; Banking and Insurance; Commerce and Economic Development.

BROCCOLI PUREE with PARMESAN & NUTMEG

3 lbs. broccoli (about 2 lg. bunches)
3/4 stick unsalted butter, cut up
2/3 C. freshly grated Parmesan cheese
1/4 tsp. ground nutmeg

Cut broccoli stems into 1-inch pieces. Cut tops into flowerettes. Bring large pot of salted water to boil. Add broccoli stems and cook 6 minutes. Add broccoli flowerettes and cook until stems and flowerettes are very tender, about 6 more minutes. Drain well. Set aside 10 flowerettes. Place remaining broccoli in processor. Add butter and puree, stopping occasionally to scrape down sides of bowl, about 5 minutes. Blend in grated Parmesan cheese and ground nutmeg. Season to taste with salt and pepper.

(Can be prepared 1 day ahead. Cover and refrigerate 10 flowerettes and broccoli puree separately. Bring flowerettes to room temperature before continuing.)

Reheat broccoli puree in saucepan. Garnish with broccoli flowerettes and serve.

Dorothy Lincoln-Smith

Dorothy Lincoln-Smith

Dorothy Lincoln-Smith has been associated with the Phoenix Boys Choir for 16 years as soprano soloist on selected programs as well as many tours in the U.S., Canada, Mexico, Europe, and the Orient. Dr. Lincoln-Smith earned music degrees at Cornell College in Iowa and at Arizona State University, and presently teaches voice at Phoenix College. She has appeared as soloist with a variety of local and national companies including the Roger Wagner Chorale.

CORN CASSEROLE SUPREME

1/2 C. butter or margarine	1 pkg. Jiffy® Corn
1 sm. onion, diced	Muffin Mix
1/2 green pepper, diced	1/4 tsp. salt
3 eggs, beaten	1/4 tsp. sugar
1 can (17 oz.) creamed style corn	1 tsp. chopped pimento
1 can (17 oz.) whole kernel	
corn, do not drain	

Top with:

1/2 pt. sour cream and 1 C. sharp cheddar cheese, grated

Heat oven to 350 degrees. Sauté butter, onion and green pepper lightly. Mix beaten eggs, 2 cans corn, muffin mix and seasonings. Pour all together with butter mixture into 9 x 13 pan. Drop spoonfuls of sour cream on top and sprinkle with cheese. Bake for 50 minutes or until done.

Ray Swanson

Ray Swanson

Ray Swanson is one of America's most distinguished painters of Native Americans of the Southwest as well as various cultures around the world. His primary interest is painting people and their environment as they struggle for survival on the land. In the last 30 years, Ray Swanson has established a successful art career and is known as a master of perspective, composition, vibrant color, and captured sunlight. Whether working in watercolor or oil, his paintings display technical understanding as well as an air of elusive softness and personal warmth. Ray has received numerous medals and honors at major art exhibitions, his most recent were a Silver Medal at the Cowboy Artists of America Show, the Bronze Medal at the International Exhibit of the American Watercolor Society, and Gold Medal in Watercolor at the 1992 Cowboy Artists of America Show. The Ray Swanson art studio is located in the desert foothills near Carefree. Ray's favorite charity in Arizona is the Christian Family Care Agency in Phoenix. For the past five years he has donated an exclusive print edition to aid the agency in its fund raising. He is the father of two adopted children. He is a member of the Western Art Associates and serves on the Board of Directors (1992-1993) in conjunction with the Phoenix Art Museum. He is a member and vice-president of the Cowboy Artists of America.

ARIZONA COWBOY BEANS

Take **four cups pinto beans**, spread out and remove the rocks. Wash 'em (the beans, not the rocks.) Soak for 24 hours, then drain and wash again. Put on to boil. Dad always said "Don't use a cast iron pot." I don't know why but he said it would tarnish the taste.

Add **ham hocks** with lots of fat. People shy away from fat these days but it adds plenty of flavor. Besides, you can scrape off the excess fat later.

Add: **one tablespoon garlic powder.**

three tablespoons black pepper.

two teaspoons of salt.

Boil three hours or more (medium boil) until the beans are soft.

Beans are one of our most essential and nutritious foods. Mankind cannot live on bread alone but he can come might close if he adds a pot of these beans to his diet now and then.

Marshall Trimble [signature]

Marshall Trimble

Marshall Trimble is an Arizona historian, cowboy singer, humorist, and storyteller. This Arizona native is one of the state's most popular and colorful personalities who is one of the most sought-after banquet and convention speakers in the state. Recently, he's been seen on ABC's "Good Morning America". He also opens for major acts performing in the Phoenix area. Marshall is considered the most widely-read chronicler of Arizona's heritage. He has written 11 books including the award-winning *Arizona: A Cavalcade of History*; *Arizona Adventure* and *In Old Arizona*. He was editor of the popular Arizona Trivia board game and script writer for the award-winning Portrait of America series on Arizona. His stories have appeared in such magazines as *Arizona Highways* and *Western Horseman*. His cassette recording, *Legends in Levis*, is a popular-selling collection of old cowboy songs. Marshall was born in Mesa in 1939 and still resides in Arizona. He is currently the director of southwest studies at Scottsdale Community College. *"An old cowboy collector and*

(continued on next page)

(Continued from previous page)

songwriter named Jack Thorp wrote a great tribute to beans back in the early 1900's."

Ode to the Bean

I've cooked you in the strongest gypsum water;
I've boiled you in water made of snow;
I've eaten you above the Arctic circle,
I've chewed on you in southern Mexico.
In the campfire, on the stove, or in the oven,
Or buried in the ashes overnight,
You've saved my life on more than one occasion . . .
Oh frijole bean, you're simply out of sight!

PASTEL DE ELOTE

1/2 lb. butter
1/2 C. sugar
4 eggs
1 can (4 oz.) green chiles
1 lb. can creamed corn
sm. jar pimentos
sm. can sliced black olives
1/2 C. grated Jack cheese
1/2 C. grated Tillamook
    cheese
1/4 tsp. salt
1 C. flour
1 C. yellow cornmeal
4 tsp. baking powder

Cream butter and sugar. Add eggs. Chop and add chiles. Mix in other ingredients. Pour into greased and floured 8 x 12 pan. Put in 350 degree oven, immediately reduce heat to 300 degrees. Bake 1 hour.

Yield: 15 servings.

Linda Thor

Linda M. Thor

Linda Thor is president of Rio Salado Community College in Phoenix.

STRAWBERRY-CREAM SQUARES

2 pkg. (3 oz.) strawberry-flavored gelatin
2 C. water, boiling
2 pkg. (10 oz.) frozen strawberries
1 can (13 1/2 oz.) crushed pineapple
2 lg. ripe bananas, finely diced
1 C. dairy sour cream

Dissolve gelatin in boiling water. Add frozen strawberries; stir occasionally till thawed. Add crushed pineapple and bananas. Pour half into 8 x 8 x 2 pan. Chill firm. Spread evenly with 1 cup sour cream. Pour remaining gelatin on top. Chill firm. Cut in 9 squares. Top with sour-cream dollops.

Dan Majerle

Dan Majerle plays guard and forward (#9) for the Phoenix Suns. He was acquired in the 1988 National Basketball Association college draft, first round, 14th overall pick. During his pro career, he has been named to the NBA's All-Defensive second team and was runner-up by one vote for the league's Sixth Man Award. Nicknamed "Thunder" for his powerful dunks and rugged inside play, Majerle provides the team with consistent offensive and defensive production regardless of whether he is starting or coming off the bench. He graduated from Central Michican University with a degree in physical education. In his spare time, Dan likes to play golf and is involved with the Stay in School program in the Phoenix area.

ARIZONA HONEY-PECAN BARS

CRUMB MIXTURE
1 1/4 C. white flour
1/3 C. sugar
1/2 C. butter
1/4 C. chopped Arizona
    pecans

FILLING
1 C. brown sugar
1/2 C. chopped Arizona pecans
1/2 C. melted butter
2 eggs
2 Tbsp. Arizona mesquite
    honey

Preheat oven to 350 degrees. Combine crumb mixture ingredients in medium mixer bowl. Beat until crumbly. Press into ungreased 9" baking pan. Bake at 350 degrees for 15 to 20 minutes. Meanwhile, in same mixer bowl, combine all filling ingredients. Beat at low speed until well mixed. Pour over hot crust. Return to oven and continue baking 25 to 30 minutes. Cool completely. Cut into bars. Yield: 2 dozen.

Barbara L. Antonsen

Lee Antonsen

Barbara L. Antonsen and Lee C. Antonsen

Both Barbara and Lee have been active in the Sedona community since moving there in 1984. They worked at helping Sedona become incorporated, then worked at establishing a new Sedona-Oak Creek School District. Lee was Sedona Citizen of the Year in 1990 and was recently re-elected to the school board. In 1989, Barbara founded the Sedona Apple Festival. (New name: Sedona Arts Festival), a non-profit organization that raises funds for Sedona's cultural organizations. This year they were able to donate $12,650 with $10,000 going to build a new cultural park. Lee and Barbara are both on the new Cultural Park board. Both are active in many other cultural organizations.

CATER LEE'S CHOCOHOLIC BARS

CRUST

1 1/2 C. flour
1 1/2 C. butter, melted
1 1/2 C. pecans, crushed

Mix above ingredients and press into 13 x 9 baking dish. Cook in 400 degree oven for 20 minutes or until golden brown. Cool 20 minutes.

TOPPING

8 oz. cream cheese
2 C. Cool Whip®

Mix and spread on crust. Then mix:

2 lg. boxes chocolate instant pudding mix
4 C. milk

Let thicken just a bit and pour on top. Then top with:

2 C. Cool Whip®
chocolate bar

Garnish with chocolate bar shavings, refrigerate and serve cold.

Cater Lee

Cater Lee is a news anchor and reporter for KTVK-TV, Channel 3 News, in Phoenix. "I'm originally from Atlanta, Georgia (Cater is an old Southern family name) and my husband and I have one 'child' - our cocker spaniel, Elvis."

CHOCOLATE ICE BOX DESSERT

1 1/2 lb. chocolate almond bars
4 eggs, separated
1/2 pt. whipping cream (I use more to make sure
   the loaf is covered)
1 1/2 to 2 dozen lady fingers (my pan uses 2)

Melt chocolate in double boiler. Beat egg yolks, add to chocolate and cook about 30 minutes until oily and gummy. Let cool, but not cold. Add to stiffly beaten egg whites.

Line loaf pan with waxed paper strips. (I do it the easy way: I bought myself a loaf pan that has removable sides and bottom.) Split lady fingers and line bottom of pan. Then alternate chocolate mixture and lady fingers. End with lady fingers on top. Cover and refrigerate for 24 hours. Remove from pan and cover with whipped cream. I put fresh holly on top.

Yield: 12 to 15.

Bill Torrey

Bill Torrey

Bill Torrey has lived in Arizona since the mid '50s. Bill is a state planner and certified public accountant and semi-retired which means he enjoys playing a lot of golf. He and his wife, Carol, have three grown children and enjoy sailing, travel, and most recently love the "Cheers" episodes. Why, you ask? It seems as though Carol won an appearance for Bill to appear on "Cheers" when she was at a COMPAS (Combined Metropolitan Phoenix Arts and Sciences) auction. The Torreys flew to Burbank for Bill's debut and he pulled up the pants of Cliff (John Ratzenberger) and teased Dr. Frasier Crane (Kelsey Grammer) about his drug stash. Carol is going to have a hard time coming up with a present to outdo her last. COMPAS raises funds through events such as this auction to provide support for the artistic and cultural needs of metropolitan Phoenix including The Heard Museum, Phoenix Art Museum, Phoenix Symphony, and the Phoenix Zoo. Oh, and you might like to know that this recipe is their traditional Christmas dessert. It has now been passed on to the third generation.

PINNACLE PEAK PERFECTION

TOPPING

1 - 14 oz. can sweetened condensed milk
1 tsp. vanilla extract
1 egg
1 - 3 1/2 oz. can (1 1/3 C.) flaked coconut divided
1 C. chopped pecans
1 - 6 oz. package (1 C.) Nestle® Toll House Semi-Sweet
  Chocolate Morsels

In large bowl, combine sweetened condensed milk, vanilla extract and egg; beat until well blended. Stir in 1 cup coconut, pecans and chocolate morsels. Set aside.

BASE

One box of brownie mix

Preheat oven to 350 degrees. In large bowl, combine brownie mix as directed on box. Pour into greased 13 x 9 inch baking pan. Spread topping over base. Sprinkle remaining 1/3 cup coconut on top. Bake at 350 degrees for 30 to 40 minutes.

Note: Center may appear loose but will set upon cooling. Cool completely on wire rack. Cut into 2" squares.

J. D. Hayworth

J. D. Hayworth is sports anchor for KTSP-TV, Channel 10 News, in Phoenix. *"This confection is 'Kryptonite' to this Superman."*

MIRLITON DE PARIS

Preheat oven to 350 degrees.

1 C. dried Turkish apricots, chopped
1/2 C. clover honey
1/3 C. hazelnuts, lightly toasted, and chopped
5 oz. Grand Marnier

1 1/4 C. almonds, ground fine
1 1/4 C. granulated sugar
4 eggs, lightly beaten
3/4 C. sweet butter, melted & browned to light walnut color
2 egg yolks

Apricot layer: mix apricots, honey and hazelnuts. Work them together thoroughly and wet with 1/2 cup of Grand Marnier. Let marinate. Almond layer: combine almonds and sugar. Gradually work in the eggs, then gradually mix as much of the browned butter as is needed to make a workable consistency.

Lightly grease with butter (or vegetable spray) a 9-inch spring-form cake pan. Spread apricot layer and pour almond layer on top. Bake in center of oven until it is all softly firm, usually in 45 to 55 minutes. (Tester should come out clean.)

GLAZE: Beat the two egg yolks with the remaining Grand Marnier. When the cake is almost done, use a pastry brush to paint its top with the yellow egg-liqueur mixture. Return cake to oven for about 5 minutes. Serve at room temperature.

Robert Shields

Robert Shields has been described by Marcel Marceau as the "greatest mime in America", His partner, Lorene Yarnell (see Lorene's recipe on page 172), describes him as *"Arizona's own one-man entertainment factory"*. He has travelled the world with his performances. His mask crafts are sold in 70 U.S. galleries. Janet Fontaine, Robert's secretary, cooks his favorite dishes and is a graduate of the Cordon Bleu Cooking School in Paris.

AUNT ROSE'S CARROT CAKE

2 C. grated carrots
1 C. vegetable oil
4 eggs, slightly beaten
1/2 C. orange honey
3/4 C. brown sugar, packed
1 tsp. cinnamon

1/2 tsp. grated orange rind
1/2 tsp. salt
1 tsp. baking soda
2 C. sifted flour
1/2 to 3/4 C. orange juice

Mix all ingredients together. When well mixed (do not beat), pour into well greased baking mold. Bake in preheated 350 degree oven on center rack for 50 to 60 minutes or until springy to touch. The carrot ring will be moist but will slice well when slightly cooled.

Ruth Solomon

Ruth Solomon of Tucson is in the Arizona House of Representatives representing District 14. The 41st Legislature (1993-1994) Directory lists her occupation as teacher. Committee assignments are: Education; Public Institutions; Ways & Means.

FRESH APPLE CAKE

2 C. sugar
8 Tbsp. shortening
2 C. flour
2 tsp. soda
1 tsp. salt
1 tsp. cinnamon
1 tsp. nutmeg

4 C. chopped apples
(Pippens)
1 C. raisins
1 C. nuts
2 tsp. vanilla
2 eggs

Mix in order given. Bake in 9 x 13 glass pan at 325 degrees for 45 minutes.

Quentin V. Tolby

Quentin Tolby is the mayor of the city of Glendale.

RUM BRANDY APPLE CAKE

1 1/3 C. sugar
1/2 C. canola oil
4 egg whites
1/4 C. rum
1/4 C. brandy
2 C. flour
1/2 tsp. cinnamon
2 tsp. baking soda
1/2 tsp. ground cloves
1/2 tsp. nutmeg

1/3 C. chopped walnuts,
    toasted 8-10 minutes
    at 350 degrees
1/2 C. raisins
4 C. apples, peeled, cored
    and sliced, or 1 (20 oz.)
    can unsweetened apples
1/4 C. fruit-only strawberry jam
1 tsp. rum

In large mixing bowl, combine sugar, oil, egg whites, rum and brandy. In separate bowl, combine flour, cinnamon, baking soda, cloves, nutmeg, walnuts and raisins. Add dry to liquid ingredients and stir until just moistened. Add apples and stir. Pour batter into a bundt pan generously sprayed with non-stick vegetable coating. Bake in 350 degree oven for 1 hour.

Remove from oven and cool 10 minutes in pan. Remove cake from pan and cool on wire rack. While cake is cooling, melt strawberry jam over low heat. Add rum, mix well and drizzle over cake.

Yield: 15 servings.

James J. Sossaman

James J. Sossaman

James Sossaman of Higley is a former Arizona state senator representing District 30. The 40th Legislature (1991-1992) Directory lists his occupation as farmer. Committee assignments were: Education; Government; Natural Resources and Agriculture.

ROCKY ROAD ANGEL FOOD CAKE

2 pkg. chocolate chips
2 Tbsp. sugar
3 egg yolks
3 egg whites
1 pt. whipping cream
angel food cake
nuts

Melt chocolate chips and sugar over hot water.

Beat egg yolks and gradually add to the chocolate mixture. Cool 5 minutes.

Beat egg whites until stiff and fold into the chocolate mixture.

Beat 1 pint whipping cream and fold into mixture. Line 8 x 12 x 2 buttered pan with bite-sized angel food cake. This should be torn with 2 forks to keep cake light. Cover cake with layer of sauce, and repeat layering, ending with sauce on top. Sprinkle with nuts and let set overnight.

This will serve from 14 to 16 people. Serve in small pieces, as it is very rich, but very delicious!

Lela Steffey

Lela Steffey of Mesa is in the Arizona House of Representatives representing District 29. The 41st Legislature (1993-1994) Directory lists her occupation as legislator/real estate. Committee Assignments are: Transportation, Chair; Banking & Insurance, Ways & Means.

SNOW PUDDING

1 Tbsp. unflavored gelatin	1/4 tsp. salt
1/2 C. cold water	1/4 C. lemon juice
3/4 C. boiling water	1 tsp. grated lemon rind
3/4 C. sugar	2 egg whites, stiffly beaten

Soften gelatin in cold water. Add boiling water, sugar and salt. Stir until dissolved. Add lemon juice and rind. Chill until mixture is slightly thicker than consistency of unbeaten egg whites. Place bowl in ice water. Continue beating until mixture begins to hold its shape. Pour into molds and chill until firm. Top with sauce or fruit.

Ray S. Parks Jr.

Ray is the president of the American Sign Language Bi-Cultural Institute and a strong advocate for the enhancement of the deaf community. In 1993 he founded DeafWorks Theatre, a non-profit professional theatre company which, using ASL, integrates deaf, deaf-blind and hearing performers in drama.

THIS IS MY FAVORITE DESSERT

CAKE
1 box yellow cake mix
4 eggs
1/4 C. oil
1 can mandarin oranges with juice
TOPPING
1 can crushed pineapple with juice (regular size)
1 pkg. instant vanilla pudding
1 (12 oz.) carton Cool Whip®

Mix cake ingredients and bake in three 8" layer pans at 350 degrees for 20 minutes. Let cool. Put topping between layers and on top and sides. Refrigerate.

Dale Johnson

Dale Johnson is a city council member for the city of Mesa.

AUNT BETTY'S INCREDIBLE CARROT CAKE

2 C. sifted flour whole
    wheat, white or both
2 C. sugar
2 tsp. soda
1 tsp. salt
4 eggs

2 tsp. cinnamon
3 C. grated carrots
1 1/2 C. vegetable oil
optional: nuts, raisins,
    pineapple

Mix all of the ingredients together and bake in 9 x 13 pan in 350 degree oven for 45-60 minutes.

FROSTING
8 oz. cream cheese
1 cube butter

1 box powdered sugar
1 tsp. vanilla

Cathy Van Camp

Cathy Van Camp

Cathy Van Camp is vice president of Northern Trust Bank and is network chair for Valley Leadership in Phoenix.

PETER'S BIRTHDAY CAKE

1 box angel food cake mix
2 pkgs. chocolate pudding, cooked
1 pt. whipped cream

Cook angel food cake in big oven-proof bowl. Turn bowl upside down to cool. When cool, cut crosswise into three layers. Fill layers with chocolate pudding. Cover all with whipped cream. Chill. Decorate with fresh flowers and candles and serve.

Peter H. Douglas

Peter Douglas

Peter Douglas is the former president of Tucson Leadership. This wonderful recipe was specifically designed for Peter's birthday.

SUE ELLEN'S JACK DANIELS CAKE

1 C. chopped pecans
1 pkg. light yellow cake mix
1 pkg. sugar-free instant
   vanilla pudding

3/4 C. Jack Daniels®
   whiskey
3/4 C. water
3 eggs

Spray bundt pan with non-stick cooking spray. Sprinkle pecans on bottom to layer. Mix together (in Cuisinart® or mixer) cake mix, pudding, water, and Jack Daniels. Beat in eggs one at a time. Pour batter into pan. Bake in 325 degree oven for 1 hour. Puffs up high.

SAUCE

1 C. margarine
3/4 C. sugar

1/4 C. water
1/4 C. Jack Daniels

Boil margarine, sugar, water and Jack Daniels. Pour over warm cake in the pan. It will soak in. Let cool completely overnight before removing from pan.

Sue Ellen

Sue Ellen Allen

Sue Ellen Allen is a Phoenix fashion jewelry designer, a motivational speaker and poet. She uses her poetry to market her jewelry to women *"who are just like me—who want accessories that make them feel beautiful both inside and out. For them and for me, my jewelry is an adornment for the body and my poetry is an accessory for the soul"*. Her jewelry commissions include The Duchess of Kent and Doc Severinson. The Congressional Club assigned her the task of creating a pin especially designed for Barbara Bush representing "A Thousand Points of Light at Christmas". Sue Ellen accessorizes the wardrobes of Laurin Sydney of CNN's "Showbiz" and Shawn Southwick of USA Network's "Hollywood Insider". Mary Hart and Leeza Gibbons of "Entertainment Tonight", "ABC Good Morning America's" Chantal, Roseanne Barr, and "All My Children's" Judy Collins wear her designs on and off the air. Sue Ellen is sold in Saks Fifth Avenue and other upscale stores and boutiques across America.

EASY CHOCOLATE DESSERT CAKE

1-9 oz. chocolate cake mix (or your own recipe)
1-8 oz. cream cheese, softened
2 C. milk (separated into halves)
1-4 oz. pkg. instant chocolate pudding mix
1-8 oz. carton whipping cream
2-4 Tbsp. sugar (to taste)
1/2 tsp. vanilla extract
2 pkg. Knox® gelatin mix*

Make cake and pour into greased and floured 13 x 9 x 2 pan and bake. Let cake cool in pan.

Place cream cheese in large mixing bowl. Gradually add in 1 cup milk, beating constantly. Add in pudding mix and remaining 1 cup milk still beating constantly. Beat until smooth and thickened. Spread evenly on top of cooled cake and set aside.

Combine whipping cream, sugar and vanilla. Whip until stiff peaks form. (*Note: Add up to 2 packages of Knox gelatin mix while whipping to get stiff peaks.) This mixture should be thick enough that it does not easily fall out of bowl if turned upside down.

Spread evenly over pudding layer. Chill and serve.

Optional: Sprinkle 2 to 4 tablespoons of almonds or chocolate chips on top.

Mark West

Mark West plays center (#41) for the Phoenix Suns. West completed his eighth season in the NBA in 1990-91, and was voted the Suns Outstanding Defensive Player in 1988-89 averaging 7.2 points and 6.7 rebounds in 82 games. He has a B.S. in Finance from Old Dominion University. Mark is very active in the Arizona community working with underprivileged kids, donating his time to clinics and camps. In his free time, Mark likes to travel. Mark and his wife, Elaina, were married in 1990. A note from Elaina: *"He enjoys this scrumptious dessert when he does eat them. He is not real big on dessert; just in size (6'10"). For a fast energy burst, 'Easy Chocolate Dessert Cake' is his favorite!"*

PIÑA COLADA PUDDING CAKE

1/3 C. Bacardi® dark rum	4 eggs
1 sm. pkg. instant pudding	1/2 C. water*
(vanilla or coconut cream)	1/4 C. oil
1 pkg. white cake mix	1 C. flaked coconut

Blend all ingredients except coconut in large mixer bowl. Beat 4 minutes at medium speed on electric mixer. Pour into 2 greased and floured 9-inch layer pans. Bake at 350 degrees for 25-30 minutes or until cakes spring back when lightly pressed. Do not underbake. Cool in pans 15 minutes; remove and cool on racks. Spread first layer with frosting, then add second layer and frost entire cake. Sprinkle with coconut. Chill. Refrigerate leftover cake.

*With vanilla flavor instant pudding and pie filling, increase water amount to 3/4 cup and add 1 cup flaked coconut to batter.

Piña Colada Frosting

1- 8 oz. can crushed pineapple
1 pkg. (4-serving size) Jello® Coconut
   Cream or Vanilla Pudding
1/3 C. Bacardi® dark rum
1- 9 oz. frozen whipped topping (thawed)

Combine pineapple (with juice), pudding mix and rum; beat until well blended; fold in whipped topping.

Jane Dee Hull

Jane Dee Hull

Jane Dee Hull of Phoenix is the former Speaker of the Arizona House of Representatives. She is currently the state representative for District 18. The 41st Arizona Legislature (1993-1994) Directory lists her occupation as homemaker. Committee assignments are: Economic Development; International Trade & Tourism, Chair; Education; Ways & Means.

BANANA CHEESE CAKE

Preheat oven to 350 degrees.

1 ten-inch pie crust pre-baked for 10 minutes
1 C. cream cheese (8 oz.)
2 1/2 C. pureed bananas (4 lg. or 6 sm. bananas)
1 1/2 C. plain yogurt (12 oz.)
2 eggs (optional)
1/4 C. honey (optional)

Blend all the ingredients in a blender until smooth and creamy. Pour into the pre-baked pie crust and bake for 30 minutes or until set. Refrigerate, and serve topped with a layer of yogurt and/or decorated with any fresh fruit (try a mixture of strawberry and banana slices).

S. Silverstone

Sally Silverstone

Sally Silverstone is the co-captain of the Biosphere 2 crew. "The crew sealed inside Biosphere 2 for two years faced a unique culinary challenge: to create delicious, varied meals using only foods from our half-acre farm and tiny barnyard. Desserts were truly a test of our creativity, since we lacked all the usual high-fat, high-sugar ingredients. You'll soon see why this cheese cake became a crew favorite! From a nutritional point of view it is very low-calorie compared with other cheese cakes, the eggs are optional (it will set perfectly well without any), and you can use fat-free cream cheese and still get a creamy texture. 'Eating In: The Biosphere 2 Cookbook' contains much more of the nutritious, low calorie cuisine which sustains and delights us in a world where you can never go out to dinner! It is scheduled to be in bookstores by fall, 1993 and it will be published by The Biosphere Press."

TOM'S FAVORITE BANANA CAKE

1 1/2 C. sugar	1 tsp. baking soda
2 eggs	1/2 tsp. salt
1/2 C. cooking oil	1/3 C. buttermilk *
1 tsp. vanilla	3/4 C. smashed bananas
2 C. flour	1/2 C. chopped walnuts

Blend first four ingredients well. Add sifted flour, baking soda and salt. Then add milk. Blend together well. Then fold in bananas and nuts. Bake in two round cake pans at 375 degrees for 35 to 40 minutes. Test with toothpick at 35 minutes to see if toothpick comes out clean. If so, cake is done. Remove to racks and let cool.

*Add 1 1/2 caps of vinegar to 1/3 C. regular milk to make substitute for buttermilk)

Seven-Minute White Icing

Place in the top of a double boiler and beat until thoroughly blended:

2 unbeaten egg whites
1 1/2 C. sugar
5 Tbsp. cold water
1/4 tsp. cream of tartar
1 1/2 tsp. light corn syrup

Place these blended ingredients over rapidly boiling water. Beat them at high speed for seven minutes. Remove from heat and add **1 tsp. vanilla**. Continue beating until icing is right consistency to spread. Spread first layer with frosting, then **fresh banana slices**. Put second layer over top and finish frosting.

Tom Agnos

Tom Agnos

Tom Agnos is the former sheriff of Maricopa County.

ARIZONA SHEETCAKE

Sift into bowl:
2 C. sugar
2 C. flour
1/2 tsp. salt

Bring to a boil and add immediately:
2 cubes butter
1 C. water
4 Tbsp. cocoa

Add to above ingredients and blend:
1/2 C. sour cream
2 eggs
1 tsp. baking soda

Pour into a sheetcake pan and bake in preheated 375 degree oven for 25 minutes

Cocoa Butter Nut Frosting

6 Tbsp. milk   **1 tsp. vanilla**
1 cube butter   **1 1 lb. box powdered sugar**
4 Tbsp. cocoa   **1 C. nuts**

Boil milk, butter, and cocoa; stir in vanilla and sugar. Blend till smooth. Fold in nuts. Spread over hot cake.

Pat Blake

Pat Blake

Pat Blake of Mesa represents District 29 in the Arizona House of Representatives. The 41st Arizona Legislature (1993-1994) Directory lists her occupation as legislator. Committee assignments are: Human Services, Chair; Banking & Insurance; Economic Development; International Trade & Tourism.

DAYBREAK DELIGHT

BATTER
1 box yellow cake mix
1 C. sour cream
1 pkg. instant vanilla pudding
   (not needed with "pudding-added mixes")
1/3 C. vegetable oil
4 eggs

TOPPING
1/2 C. sugar
1/2 C. chopped pecans
1 tsp. cinnamon
2 tsp. cocoa

Mix topping well. Set aside.

Add batter ingredients together and beat well. Grease bundt pan. Sprinkle some topping mixture on bottom of pan. Spoon some batter in, then sprinkle more sugar topping, then more batter; finish with topping. With knife, swirl through batter. Bake at 350 degrees for 45 minutes. Freezes well.

Perry R. Hubbard

Perry R. Hubbard is the mayor of the city of Litchfield Park.

JEWISH APPLE CAKE

3 C. flour
2 C. sugar
4 eggs
1 C. oil
1 tsp. salt
1/4 C. orange juice
3 tsp. baking powder

2 1/2 tsp. vanilla
5-6 apples, pared, sliced
(or canned pie sliced
apples, drained
2 tsp. cinnamon
5 tsp. sugar

In large bowl combine all ingredients except apples, cinnamon and sugar. Beat until smooth (about 2 to 3 minutes) at medium speed. Pour 1/2 batter into a 10-inch tube cake or bundt pan that is greased and floured.

Combine apples, cinnamon and sugar. Add 1/2 apple mixture over batter in pan. Spread rest of batter on top of apple mixture and top with remaining apple mix. If desired, sprinkle walnuts or pecans on top. Bake in 350 degree oven for 1 1/4 to 1 1/2 hours. Cool. Serve with whipped cream or ice cream.

George Miller

George Miller

George Miller is the mayor of the city of Tucson. Born in Detroit, he first came to Tucson in 1939 where he attended Tucson High School. Following the war, Miller resumed his education at the University of Arizona and graduated in 1947 with a Bachelor of Science degree and in 1952 received his Master of Education. After seven years as a teacher, he worked his way up through the painting trade eventually owning his own business until retirement in 1989. In his fourth term with the Tucson City Council he ran successfully for mayor. Awards include Man of the Year (Southern Arizona Home Builders Association), Certificate of Appreciation from San Ignacio Yaqui Council, Old Pasqua, a two-time recipient of the Community Services Award - Chicanos Por La Causa, Recognition Award from United Way, LULAC Award for service to Hispanic community and the Labor Movement. He has served on the Tucson Jewish Community Center Board for twelve years. He added this light-hearted note, "*A hunk of this cake - and you can't be mad at anyone!*"

CARAMELS

2 C. white sugar
3/4 C. light Karo® Syrup
1/4 lb. butter
1 pt. thick (whipping) cream

Put sugar, syrup, butter and 1 cup (1/2 of pint) cream over medium heat and stir until boiling thoroughly. Gradually stir in the remaining cream, slowly, so that boiling does not stop. Put thermometer in and stir until temperature reaches 240 to 250 depending on the thermometer. Take off heat and stir in one **Tbsp. vanilla**. Pour into well buttered 8 x 12 or 9 x 13 pan. Cool overnight on counter and cut and wrap each piece in waxed paper.

Sue Gilbertson

Sue Gilbertson

Sue Gilbertson is the founder of M.I.K.I.D.(Mentally Ill Kids In Distress), an organization of parents and other family members with concerns for children and adolescents who have neurobiological disorders and related behavioral health problems. The group started in 1987 with only five families and has grown to over 750 families statewide in Tucson, Yuma, Flagstaff, Cottonwood, Kingman, and Prescott. Sue was the recipient of the 1992 Community Award from TERROS, a behavioral health service.

MAMINKA'S RUSSIAN COOKIES

Mix the following ingredients together to make a fairly stiff dough:

2 1/4 sticks butter
1 1/2 C. sugar
2 1/2 C. flour
8 oz. finely-ground
  almond meal

1 Tbsp. lemon juice
I lemon (the grated peel)
dash of vanilla (to taste)
dash of cinnamon (to taste)
pinch of salt

Roll out dough and cut one batch of it with a round cookie-cutter, another batch with a doughnut cutter. Bake at 375 degrees for 10 to 12 minutes. Remove from oven and let cool. Spread the round cookies with a teaspoon each of your favorite jam. Sprinkle the doughnut cookies with confectioners sugar, and place them on top of the others so that the jam shows nicely in the middle. Just remember to make plenty; they go fast.

Aliza Caillou

Aliza Caillou

Aliza Caillou appeared in the *Red Rock News* in Sedona on December 13, 1991 featuring samples of her bead work. The adventures of Aliza Caillou, 79, and her husband Alan Caillou, are countless. From the *Red Rock News*: "Caillou's exploits rival the imaginary exploits of the film character Indiana Jones." Her journey began in the Middle East. She spoke nine languages but says she only speaks six now, she's forgotten her Arabic and Swahili. She studied in London, worked in Palestine, and enlisted in the British Army when Hitler invaded Poland in September, 1939. She worked in counterintelligence and volunteered as assistant to the political intelligence officer in Cairo. During this time, all the allied women were being shipped to South Africa. During her journey, she convinced the captain to let her go to Kenya. From there, she began her journey to Asmara. Aliza traveled the Nile by boat and experienced arrows and spears cross-firing from tribal wars. She searched for her husband, who had been declared missing in action and eventually found him. After the war, the couple went to England and then to Africa. They now live in Arizona. Aliza enjoys bead work, ceramics, cake decorating, candy making, stamp collecting, playing chess and going to garage sales.

NAPOLEON SQUARE COOKIES

1 pkg refrigerator chocolate
   chip cookie dough
   (largest size)
1 - 8 oz. pkg. cream cheese

1 egg
1/3 C. sugar
1 tsp. vanilla

Grease a 9-inch square pan well. Slice package of cookies into 1/4 inch slices. Line pan with 1/2 of the cookies and pat down. Bake 15 minutes at 350 degrees. Remove from oven and let cool for 25 minutes. Whip cream cheese, egg, sugar and vanilla until creamy. Spread over bottom layer. Cover with remaining cookies. Sprinkle **chopped nuts** over top. Bake at 350 degrees for 25 minutes. Let cool and cut into squares. Yield: 1 dozen.

Bruce Kirk

Bruce Kirk is news anchor for KPNX-TV, Channel 12 News, in Phoenix.

CREAMY FUDGE

1 pkg. (6 oz.) chocolate chips
1/3 stick butter
2 C. powdered sugar
1/4 C. sour cream

1 Tbsp. cherry juice
2 Tbsp. chopped cherries
1 tsp. vanilla
1 C. nuts

Melt chips and butter in double boiler. Add sugar (remove from heat), sour cream, cherry juice, cherries, vanilla and nuts. Blend well. Turn into buttered 8 x 8 pan. Cool, cut into 1-inch squares.

Mickey Ollson

Mickey Ollson is director of the Wildlife World Zoo in Litchfield Park, which features a variety of exotic animals on a 40-acre park.

CHEESE CAKE COOKIES

CRUST
1/3 C. butter, cold
1/3 C. brown sugar, packed
1 C. flour

Mix well. Use 2 knives to cut through or use pastry blender to make a crumb mixture. Reserve 1/2 cup crumbs. Press remaining crumbs evenly into 8-inch square pan. Bake in 350 degree oven 10 to 12 minutes.

FILLING

1 pkg. (8 oz.) cream cheese
1/3 C. sugar
1 Tbsp. lemon juice

1 egg
1/3 C. each chopped
red and green cherries

Beat first 4 ingredients together well. Fold in cherries. Pour over crust. Sprinkle with remaining crumbs. Bake in 350 degree oven for 25 to 30 minutes.

Jineane Ford
Jineane Ford is news anchor for KPNX-TV Channel 12, in Phoenix.

LADMO'S POLISH KURSZCZYKI
(pronounced CRUS-CHICKIES)

1 Tbsp. sugar
1 tsp. vanilla
1 carton (16 oz.) sour cream
6 eggs (1 whole egg, 5 yellow yolks)
4 to 5 cups flour, sifted

    Mix sugar, vanilla, sour cream and eggs with eggbeater. Add flour (more if needed to roll). Mix with hands; knead. Let rest for about 15 minutes, then roll like a pie crust but thin. Work slow. Cut in long strips about 1 1/2 inches wide and 5 inches long. Make cut in center. Pull both ends through slit, to create a bow. Drop each one in deep fryer (Crisco® works best) for just a few seconds, until lightly browned only. Lay on paper towels or newspaper to dry. After cooling, sprinkle with powdered sugar.

Ladmo

Ladmo

    Ladmo is half of the KPHO Channel 5, Wallace & Ladmo team. Ladmo writes, "*My mother always made these at Christmastime and they are so-o-o-o good. She is now teaching my children and grandchildren how to make them, so they will always be a family favorite.*"

OATMEAL CRISPIES

1 C. shortening
1 C. brown sugar
1 C. white sugar
2 eggs
1 tsp. vanilla
1 1/2 C. flour
1 tsp. salt
1 tsp. soda
3 C. quick cooking oatmeal
1/2 C. chopped walnuts

Cream shortening and sugars (brown and white). Add eggs and vanilla and beat well. Add sifted dry ingredients (flour, salt, and soda), oatmeal and nuts and mix well. Shape into rolls, wrap in wax paper and chill overnight. Slice into 1/4 inch pieces.

Bake on ungreased cookie sheets at 350 degrees for 10 minutes.

Lela Alston

Lela Alston

Lela Alston of Phoenix is an Arizona state senator representing District 20. The 41st Arizona Legislature (1993-1994) Directory lists her occupation as educator. Committee assignments are: Appropriations; Education; Government; Rules.

MEATBALL COOKIES

5 C. flour	1/2 tsp. salt
1 1/2 C. sugar	1 C. shortening,
1 C. cocoa	melted and cooled
2 tsp. cinnamon	2 C. milk
2 tsp. cloves	1 C. raisins
1 tsp. nutmeg	1 C. chocolate chips
1 tsp. baking soda	1 C. chopped walnuts
2 tsp. baking powder	

Mix dry ingredients; add shortening and stir; add milk and stir. Add raisins, chocolate chips and walnuts and blend well. You will need to use your hands at this point. Roll into balls of desired size, greasing hands if necessary. Bake on ungreased cookie sheets in 350 degree oven for 7 minutes on the upper rack and 7 minutes on the lower rack. Cool and frost with a thin confectioners' glaze.

Yield: 60 large cookies.

Carol A. Shiery

Carol A. Shiery

Carol Shiery is a special education teacher at Flagstaff Junior High School as well as special olympics activities events director in Arizona Special Olympics Winter Games. Carol is also coach for state level competition in aquatics, bowling, cross country skiing, athletics, team handball, volleyball and equestrian. She was coach for Team Arizona Athletics VII International Summer Special Olympics Games in Indiana in 1987 and for the VII Games in Minnesota in 1991. In 1987 she received from the Northern Arizona University, Master of Arts Degree in Education, Special Education Mental Retardation 1979, Bachelor of Science Degree in Art Education.

HAPPY DAY CUPCAKES

1 stick margarine or butter
    (softened at room temperature)
2 1/4 C. flour (all-purpose)
3 tsp. baking powder
1 tsp. salt
1 1/2 C. sugar
1 C. milk
2 eggs, unbeaten (room temperature)
1 tsp. flavoring (vanilla or lemon)

Stir margarine or butter. Sift in dry ingredients. Add 3/4 cup milk. Mix until flour is dampened. Beat 2 minutes. Add eggs, flavoring, and remaining milk. Mix well. Pour into 2 greased muffin pans. Bake in 375 degree oven for 25 minutes.

Yield: 24 medium cupcakes.

Coy Payne

Coy Payne

Coy Payne is the mayor of the city of Chandler. He became Chandler's 28th mayor on March 8, 1990 and was re-elected to his second term on January 21, 1992. He served eight years on the City Council, the last two as vice mayor. Payne is the first black mayor of an Arizona city. He has an extensive public service record: director of the Maricopa Association of Governments, Regional Public Transportation Authority, Arizona Municipal Waters Users Association, Chandler Regional Hospital Foundation Advisory Board, Salvation Army Board, and a member of the Greater Phoenix Economic Council, League of Arizona Cities & Towns and Chandler Rotary Club. Payne has lived in Chandler for 49 years and he and his wife Willie have six children.

Dolly's Mud Pie

3 tbl spoons dirt
1 mouthful water
Blend ~~ingridience~~
~~ingreedent~~
the stuff
together. Then squish
around for two
minutes, and serve
to your little brother.

Bil Keane

Bil Keane

Bil Keane draws the internationally syndicated cartoon "*The Family Circus*", which apears in 1,400 newspapers and is read by 100 million people daily. Three animated holiday specials have appeared on NBC television, and the feature adorns many licensed products. "*The Family Circus*" started in 1960. The ideas and characters were based on Keane's own family. Many grammar schools across the nation display specially drawn "*Family Circus*" posters that promote reading, self esteem, respect for teachers, etc. Bil became president of the National Cartoonist Society in 1981. He has won many awards, including the highest honor cartoonists can bestow on their peers, the prestigious Reuben Award.

BANANA CREAM PIE

2 C. milk	2 Tbsp. butter or margarine
3/4 C. sugar	1 pie crust, baked
1/3 C. flour	2 bananas
1/8 tsp. salt	2 stiffly-beaten egg whites
2 well-beaten egg yolks	4 Tbsp. sugar
1/2 tsp. vanilla	

Scald milk. Mix dry ingredients. Pour gradually into scalded milk. Cook until mixture thickens. Pour gradually over the two beaten egg yolks. Cook five minutes more. Add vanilla and butter. Cool.

Place 1/2 creme filling into baked pie shell. Cover with sliced bananas. Add remaining filling. Cover with meringue made of stiffly-beaten egg white to which sugar has been added. Brown in 300 degree oven for 20 minutes.

Microwave instructions:

Heat milk. Add dry ingredients. Stir occasionally. Add beaten egg yolks. Cook until thick. Remove from microwave. Add butter or margarine and vanilla. Stir. Cool. Add to pie crust, add bananas and meringue, and bake same as above.

Jim Bruner

Jim Bruner

Jim Bruner is the chairman of the Maricopa County Board of Supervisors, District 2.

MOM'S PUMPKIN PIE

"My favorite dessert is pumpkin pie, and the best of those I ever tasted were baked by my mother, Cevilia. She baked them all her life, even for family gatherings when she was in her nineties."

1 1/2 C. sugar	1 can pumpkin
1 tsp. salt	3 C. milk
1 tsp. ginger	1 can evaporated milk
1 Tbsp. flour	4 eggs, well-beaten
4 tsp. cinnamon	pie crust

Mix ingredients well, pour into pie crust and bake in 425 degree oven for 15 minutes, then in 350 degree oven for 45 minutes.

Charles D. Lauer

Charles D. Lauer

Charles Lauer is a western writer and photographer. He has two books in print, *Old West Adventures in Arizona* and *Tales of Arizona Territory*. Lauer is a native of Iowa and was stationed at Luke Air Field and Douglas Air Base in Arizona while serving in the Army Air Force during World War II. He received his B.A. and M.A. degrees in education at Arizona State University. While earning his living by selling real estate in Arizona, his principal avocation was researching Arizona history and visiting Arizona historical sites. He was music director and has written music for the choir at his church.

GRANDMA'S CHOCOLATE PIE

1 C. sugar
4 heaping Tbsp. cocoa
1/4 C. and 2 Tbsp. flour
3 eggs
2 C. milk

1 tsp. vanilla
1 baked pie crust
whipped cream
1 tsp. vanilla
2 tsp. sugar

Mix sugar, cocoa and flour in saucepan. Beat eggs and milk, add to sugar mixture. Stir over medium to high heat, stirring constantly until bubbling. Add vanilla. Pour into baked pie crust. Top with whipped cream flavored with vanilla and sugar.

Grant Woods

Grant Woods is the attorney general for the State of Arizona.

CREAM CHEESE PIE

4 pkg. (3 oz.) cream cheese
2 eggs
3/4 C. sugar
2 tsp. vanilla
1/2 tsp. lemon juice

Cream together, pour into **graham cracker crust**. Bake in 350 degree oven for 15-20 minutes.

TOPPING
1 C. sour cream
3 1/4 tsp. sugar
1 tsp. vanilla

Mix topping and spread on cooled pie. Bake 10 minutes. Refrigerate 5 hours. Every day is a feast. Enjoy this delicious treat.

Christi Todd

Christi Todd

Christi Todd was awarded one of the "12 Who Care Hon Kachina Awards". The Luke's Men of St. Luke's Medical and Behavioral Health Centers and KPNX Channel 12 honor twelve outstanding volunteers for their contributions to humanity. According to Indian legend, the Hon Kachina represents great healing powers. Because each of these recipients have been so giving of themselves and assisted in the healing of others, they have been awarded the Hon Kachina symbolizing excellence in volunteer service.

SODA CRACKER PIE

PIE
14 soda crackers
1 tsp. baking powder
1 C. nuts, chopped
3 egg whites
1 C. sugar
1 tsp. vanilla

TOPPING
1/2 pt. whipping cream
4 Tbsp. powdered sugar
1/2 tsp. vanilla

Crush soda crackers. Add baking powder, nuts. Whip egg whites until stiff and add sugar gradually and vanilla. Fold cracker mixture into egg mixture and pour into greased pie tin. Bake in 350 degree oven for 30 minutes. Let cool 2 hours. Whip cream until stiff. Add powdered sugar and vanilla. Spread over pie. Let stand at least 5-8 hours in refrigerator.

James P. "Jim" Stapley

Jim Stapley is a city council member for the city of Mesa.

MUD PIE

Layer 1 - CRUST

Melt:
1 1/2 cubes butter or margarine

Add:
1 1/2 C. flour
1/2 C. chopped pecans
2 Tbsp. brown sugar

Mix well. Spread in 13 x 9 pan. Bake in 350 degree oven for 20 minutes. Let cool.

Layer 2 - CREAM FILLING

Whip:
1-8 oz. pkg. cream cheese
1/2 C. sugar
1/2 (12 oz.) carton Cool Whip®

Spread on cooled crust.

Layer 3 - TOPPING

Mix: **2 (3 oz.) boxes Jello® Instant Pudding** (chocolate - made as for pie recipe)

Pour over 2nd layer. Let set.

Top with remaining Cool Whip. Sprinkle with chopped pecans and/or chocolate shavings.

Matt Salmon

Matt Salmon of Mesa is in the Arizona State Senate representing District 21. The 41st Arizona Legislature (1993-1994) Directory lists his occupation as community relations manager. Committee Assignments are: Rules, Chair; Appropriations; Finance. Matt wrote that he usually doesn't eat desserts but this one he cannot stay away from!

SOUTHERN PECAN PIE

3 eggs, beaten
2/3 C. sugar
1/3 tsp. salt
1/3 C. butter, melted
1 C. dark corn syrup or
    light corn syrup

1 C. pecans, chopped
3 Tbsp. milk
1 tsp. vanilla
unbaked pie shell

Combine ingredients and pour into pie shell. Bake in 300 degree oven for 45 minutes or until firm. Crust should be evenly browned.

Steve Owens

Steve Owens is chairman of the Arizona Democratic Party. A native Tennessean, Steve worked for many years for U.S. senator (now Vice President) Al Gore, before moving to Arizona in December 1988. Among other positions, Steve served as Gore's chief counsel in Washington, D.C., his state director in Tennessee, and the southern director on his 1988 presidential campaign. Steve is a partner in the Phoenix law firm of Brown & Bain. Steve and his wife Karen live in Phoenix with their son John, born on February 20, 1992.

MINCEMEAT CHEESE PIE

4 (3 oz.) pkg. cream cheese	2 C. mincemeat
2 eggs	baked 9-inch pastry shell
1/2 C. + 2 Tbsp. sugar	1 C. sour cream
grated peel of 1 lemon	1/2 tsp. vanilla
1 Tbsp. lemon juice	twisted lemon slices

Preheat oven to 375 degrees. Beat together cream cheese, eggs, 1/2 cup sugar, grated lemon peel and lemon juice with an electric mixer until very smooth. Spoon mincemeat into baked pastry shell. Pour cream cheese mixture over mincemeat. Bake 20 minutes. Mix together sour cream, 2 tablespoons sugar and vanilla. When pie has baked 20 minutes, remove from the oven and spread sour cream mixture evenly over top. Return to oven for 10 minutes. Then chill pie before cutting and serving. Garnish with twisted lemon slices.

Marion Pickens

Marion L. Pickens

Marion L. Pickens of Tucson formerly represented District 9 in the Arizona House of Representatives. The 40th Arizona Legislature (1991-1992) Directory lists her occupation as teacher. Committee assignments were: Commerce; Financial Insitutions and Insurance; Licensing, Professions and Tourism; Transportation. This recipe has become a Thanksgiving family tradition. Marion says she uses the brandied mincemeat that comes in a jar and she uses full calories on sour cream and cream cheese. She noted, *"I don't even want to know how many calories are in a slice"*. (Author's note: Well, Marion, we all cheat on the calories during the Thanksgiving holidays so don't give it another worry! Just enjoy!)

CHIFFON CREAM PIE

1 1/4 C. chocolate wafer crumbs
1/2 C. melted butter
1 envelope (1 Tbsp.) unflavored gelatin
1/4 C. cold water
3 eggs, separated
1/2 C. sugar
1/4 tsp. salt
1 tsp. vanilla
1 C. scalded milk
1 C. heavy cream, whipped

Combine crumbs and butter. Press firmly over bottom and sides of a greased 9-inch pie pan. Chill. Sprinkle gelatin on the cold water. Combine egg yolks, sugar, salt and vanilla; add to hot milk. Cook over hot water until mixture coats spoon. (I cook this mixture slowly over direct heat and stir constantly.) Add gelatin to hot mixture; stir until dissolved. Chill until syrupy - (almost set). Fold in stiffly beaten egg whites and whipped cream. Pour into pie pan that was lined with crumb crust. Garnish with additional chocolate wafer crumbs. Chill until firm. Enjoy!

Betsy Douglas

Betsy Douglas

Betsy Douglas is a self-employed designer and metalsmith who makes fine art jewelry. She also is a freelance writer for jewelry and metal publications. She has lived in Arizona for 14 years, and received her master in fine art degree in metal from Arizona State University in 1984. Her work has been included in numerous regional and national exhibitions and is represented by the Stetter Gallery in Phoenix, Arizona. Betsy is currently serving on the board of directors of the Society of North American Goldsmiths.

INDIAN PUDDING

4 C. milk
1/2 C. yellow corn meal
2 Tbsp. melted butter
1/2 C. molasses

1 tsp. salt
1 tsp. cinnamon
1/4 tsp. ginger
2 eggs

Scald milk, pour slowly on corn meal, stirring constantly. Cook over hot water 20 minutes. Combine butter, molasses, salt, cinnamon and ginger. Beat eggs, add with molasses mixture to corn meal. Pour into greased baking dish. Place in pan of hot water. Bake in 350 degree oven for 1 hour. Serve hot with hard sauce, plain or whipped cream, or vanilla ice cream. Yield: Serves 6.

John M. Cutillo

John Cutillo is the mayor of Fountain Hills.

NO BAKE CHEESECAKE PIE

1- 8 oz. carton whipping cream
1 -8 oz. package cream
1 C. sour cream
1/4 C. powdered sugar

1 Tbsp. lemon juice
1 tsp. vanilla
graham cracker crust
1 can cherries

Mix first 6 ingredients in blender. Pour into prepared graham cracker pie crust. Top with cherries.

Larry K. Christiansen

Larry Christiansen is the president of Mesa Community College.

SWEET POTATO COBBLER

3 C. peeled, cubed sweet potatoes
1 C. water
1 C. sugar
1/4 C. margarine, melted
1 C. unsifted self-rising flour
3/4 C. sugar
3/4 C. milk
dash of cinnamon
dash of nutmeg

Cook sweet potatoes in water until tender in medium saucepan over medium-high flame. Stir in 1 cup sugar and set aside. Pour margarine in 8-inch square baking pan. Mix flour, 3/4 cup sugar, and milk. Pour over margarine. Spoon potatoes and syrup evenly on top of batter; do not stir. Sprinkle with cinnamon and nutmeg. Preheat over to 350 degrees. Cook 30 minutes.

Annie Brayboy

Annie Brayboy, ACSW, MSW, received double honors at Phoenix area National Association of Social Workers awards program, where she was named Social Worker of the Year in 1992 both for the branch and for the three-state Phoenix Area Indian Health Service. Brayboy, a member of the Lumbee Indian tribe of North Carolina, is director of the Gila River Indian Community Behavioral Health Program at the Hu Hu Kam Memorial Hospital in Sacaton.

OZARK PUDDING

1 egg
3/4 C. sugar
2 heaping Tbsp. flour
1 1/4 tsp. baking powder
1/4 tsp. salt

1+ tsp. vanilla
1/2 C. walnuts or pecans,
    finely chopped
1/2 C. peeled raw apples,
    chopped

Beat egg; add sugar and beat until smooth; add flour, baking powder and salt. Add vanilla, nuts and apples. Bake in greased 8 x 8 pan in 350 degree oven for 35 minutes. Serve with whipped cream.

Rudy Turk

Rudy Turk

Rudy Turk is retired after 25 years as art museum director at Arizona State University. He is a writer, critic, lecturer, professor of art and humanities, and painter.

NOODLE KUGEL

Mix together:

1 C. sugar
1 lb. cooked noodles
1 lb. cottage cheese
1 1/2 tsp. vanilla
1 C. white raisins

7 eggs
2 C. milk
1 pt. sour cream
1/8 lb. melted butter

Pour into large pan (17 x 12 x 2 or 2 smaller ones). Refrigerate overnight. When ready to bake, top with **1/2 C. crumbled cornflakes, 1 tsp. cinnamon** and **1 tsp. sugar**. Bake at 350 degrees for 1 1/2 hours or until brown on top.

Shelley Cohn

Shelley Cohn

Shelley Cohn is the executive director of the Arizona Commission on the Arts.

CHRISTMAS PLUM PUDDING

Thoroughly mix the following ingredients:
1 1/2 C. ground suet
2 C. raisins (or currants)
1 C. sugar
1 tsp. nutmeg
1 tsp. cinnamon
1 tsp. mace
1 tsp. baking soda
1/2 tsp. salt
3/4 scant C. whole milk
2 C. flour

After these ingredients are thoroughly mixed place them in a steamer and steam for at least four hours.

To make hard sauce for the plum pudding, cream **1/2 cup butter** and blend with **1 whole egg**, **1 1/2 cups powdered sugar** and **1 tsp. lemon** (or vanilla if preferred) **flavoring**, to serve on the hot plum pudding.

(I am told you can make a plum pudding in a microwave by covering it with plastic wrap and microwaving it at 7 power for 15 minutes, turning every five minutes. However, I have never tried to make it in a microwave and cannot vouch for it!)

James Moeller

James Moeller

James Moeller of Phoenix is vice chief justice of the Supreme Court.

DADDY'S PLUM PUDDING

1/2 C. margarine
2 C. flour
1 C. molasses
1 C. raisins
1 tsp. baking soda, mixed in a little warm water
1 C. pecans, chopped
1 C. buttermilk

Mix above well and steam in 6 greased cans (vegetable cans) for 3 hours.

Serve with the following:
1 C. sugar
1/2 C. margarine
4 well beaten egg yolks
1 nice glass brandy
1 lg. can evaporated milk

Cook in double boiler until light and creamy. Spoon over the plum pudding.

Warren H. Stewart, Sr.

Warren H. Stewart is the pastor of the First Institutional Baptist Church in Phoenix. He was one of six people honored in January by Coretta Scott King, widow of the Reverend Martin Luther King Jr., in Washington. Dr. Stewart served as chairman of Victory Together, a group that registered 75,000 Arizona voters as part of its campaign and was a key player in the passage of a paid King Holiday for state employees.

PUMPKIN DESSERT BREAD

"The tastiest treat in town."

1 C. butter or margarine	1/2 tsp. salt
2 C. sugar	3 tsp. ground cinnamon
1 can (1 lb.) pumpkin	1 tsp. ground mace
1/4 C. molasses	1 tsp. ground allspice
3 C. all-purpose flour	1 C. raisins
1 tsp. baking soda	1 C. pecans, chopped
1 tsp. baking powder	

Cream sugar and butter together. Add pumpkin and molasses and beat. Add flour, baking soda, baking powder, salt, cinnamon, mace and allspice and beat again. Stir in raisins and pecans. Pour batter into a lightly greased and floured tube pan and bake in a 350 degree oven for 1 hour or until tests done with a toothpick.

Serves 8 to 10.

Ellen Bilbrey

Ellen Bonnin-Bilbrey

Ellen owns an environmental public relations firm in Phoenix. Eco-logical marketing represents businesses that are trying to bring environmental products to market. She has represented many environmental non-profit organizations and helps environmental organizations including Wildlife for Tomorrow, Women's Environmental Council, Earth Day Arizona, Earth Rally, Hydrogen Association and many more.

"This recipe was first published by a former public relations person and well-known chef now living in New Mexico, Lynn Nusom. Lynn is the author of cookbooks (Christmas in Arizona, New Mexico Cook Book and The Tequila Cook Book to name a few) and he also reviews cookbooks for his syndicated newspaper column."

SOMETHING SCRUMPTIOUS SORBET

2 C. water
1 1/2 C. sugar
2 C. fresh squeezed grapefruit juice
1 C. red raspberries, pureed
1 C. cranberry juice

Put water and sugar in saucepan and bring to boil, then turn temperature to low for 5 minutes. Set aside for 10 minutes.

Mix grapefruit juice, red raspberries and cranberry juice together in freezer can, then pour sugar water into freezer. Cover and begin turning freezer for about 45 minutes or until iced or nearly frozen. Remove freezer from ice cream machine; remove paddle, lick paddle clean and pat sorbet until solid mass in freezer can. Then place in refrigerator freezer until frozen solid. Serve when ready to enjoy "something scrumptious." Call Jack Nylund to "share anytime."

Jack Nylund

Jack Nylund is the president of the Glendale Chamber of Commerce.

BANANAS FOSTER

5 Tbsp. butter
6 Tbsp. brown sugar
1/2 tsp. cinnamon
2 tsp lemon juice
4 bananas cut in half lengthwise
1/2 C. dark rum
French vanilla ice cream

Melt butter in large heavy skillet. Add brown sugar and cinnamon, stirring constantly over low heat. Add lemon juice and bananas, warming a bit. At tableside, add rum and ignite. Serve over ice cream.

Tom Purtzer

Tom Purtzer is one of Arizona's PGA members. The 41-year-old Scottsdale resident has been on the tour for 18 years. He attended Arizona State University. *"After going from city to city on the PGA Golf Tour for the past 18 years, I have had the opportunity to dine in restaurants all over the world. No matter where I am I always start with the dessert menu in hopes of finding Banana's Foster there, that way I know what to order for my entree to accommodate my sweet tooth. Unfortunately, not many restaurants offer this dessert. Since fewer and fewer places offer it, I had to take it upon myself to find my own recipe. Check out these ingredients and you'll understand why anyone with any health sense whatsoever would know that this dessert is off limits. So, under doctor's orders; play one round of golf, eat a light dinner and indulge yourself with this dessert fit for a king — and I don't mean Arnold Palmer!"*

BANANAS GLAZED with GUAVA-RUM

**1/2 C. guava jelly (or,
     substitute apple jelly)
2 Tbsp. rum (or 1 tsp.
     rum extract)
6 ripe bananas
3 Tbsp. butter
1 tsp. brown sugar
pinch of salt**

Melt the jelly with the rum over low heat and let simmer few minutes until thickened to a glazing consistency. Slice the bananas lengthwise. Melt butter in frying pan over medium heat and sauté the bananas, first on one side, then on the other. After turning the bananas, sprinkle with brown sugar and touch of salt. Sauté bananas just until they begin to brown. Serve on warm plates and glaze with the guava-rum mixture.

Yield: Serves 6 humans. Multiply the quantities by at least 10 if any of your guests are elephants.

Dick George for RUBY THE ELEPHANT

Ruby the Elephant is an internationally acclaimed artist now residing at the Phoenix Zoo. The 19 year old Asian elephant began her painting in 1987 when her trainers decided it was something she might like to do. Her paintings have sold for as much as $2500.00. Proceeds from her paintings benefit the Conservation Fund, which supports work with rare and endangered species. Bank of America now has checks with paintings by Ruby, which help provide donations for the Conservation Fund, as well. The check design is a reproduction of a portion of Ruby's painting "Smithsonian", named in honor of the magazine that featured her in December 1990. Dick George is the publications manager for The Phoenix Zoo. Dick writes, *"As Ruby's amanuensis, I am pleased to send you one of her favorite recipes for your cookbook project. Of course, Ruby herself is much too occupied pondering elephant thoughts to bother with cooking: in her view, that's one of the few things we puny humans are good for, in addition to taking dictation and handling her correspondence. At any rate here is Ruby's culinary entry."*

GOLDEN APPLE DELIGHT

10 to 12 golden delicious apples
1/2 C. (or more) cinnamon candies
sugar

Cut up and cook apples until cooked down. Add cinnamon candies until mixture turns pink. Sugar to taste. This can be served hot or cold and can be frozen.

Bill Frieder

Bill Frieder

Bill Frieder is the head basketball coach for the Sun Devils at Arizona State University. Before making his mark at ASU, Frieder coached in his native state, Michigan, and was the National Coach of the Year in 1985. The recipe of his choice is Golden Apple Delight—but the real apple of his eye is his daughter, Laura, who has been very successful in junior equestrian competition as a state champion show jumper.

KIBBLES 'N BITS

1/2 C. (1 stick) margarine
1 pkg. (12 oz.) chocolate chips
3/4 C. peanut butter
1 box Crispix® cereal
2 C. powdered sugar

Melt first 3 ingredients together in microwave oven. Empty cereal into large bowl. Pour melted mixture over cereal and mix thoroughly. Dump mixture into large paper bag with 1/2 cup powdered sugar. Shake. Repeat, adding 1/2 cup powdered sugar and shaking until 2 cups powdered sugar have been added. Serve in new dog dish to shock your friends.

Tony Walters

Tony Walters

Tony Walters was one of two Arizona athletes on Team USA in the World Winter Special Olympics in Ramsau, Austria in 1993. He cross country skiied to win a bronze medal in the 500 meter race. Tony has won many medals in Arizona Special Olympics. He competed in race walking and running in International Special Olympics competition in Minneapolis in 1991. Tony is a graduate of Marcos de Niza High School in Tempe. He was named outstanding Tempe handicapped student. He is currently employed by McDonald's in the McJobs program and was named Phoenix McJob's employee of the year for 1988. Tony's mom, Karen, wrote: *"Tony is really thrilled to be included in your cookbook. The recipe he contributed is a snack that he can make. He is such a positive and happy person that he likes this recipe for the fun you can have with it. This recipe survived most of a week of teens' camp without being raided by the other campers. Nobody wanted to eat dogfood until they tasted it. Then it was gone in a flash!"*

NIGHTY-NIGHTS

(The Ultimate bedtime snack)

2 lg. egg whites
2/3 C. sugar
1 C. chocolate chips

Preheat the oven to 325 degrees. Line 2 cookie sheets with foil and set aside. In a small bowl, beat the egg whites until foamy, gradually add the sugar, and beat on high speed until stiff peaks form. Fold in the chocolate chips and drop the batter by small teaspoonfuls onto the cookie sheets (the cookies should look like small mounds and should not be allowed to spread). Place in the oven, turn off the heat, and let sit overnight.

Note: Also delicious without the chocolate chips, these cookies may be shaped into small nests to hold fruit or flavored whipped cream. They are best stored in an air-tight tin.

Yield: 2 dozen.

Chip Weil

Louis A. Weil III

Louis A. "Chip" Weil III, is the publisher and chief executive officer for Phoenix Newspapers, Inc., publishers of *The Arizona Republic, The Phoenix Gazette* and *Arizona Business Gazette*. He is a member of the Greater Phoenix Leadership, the Cronkite Endowment Board of Trustees for the Walter Cronkite School of Journalism and Telecommunication at Arizona State University; the Board of Directors of the Foundation for American Communications; Phoenix Art Museum Board of Trustees and the Advisory Board of the Arizona Cancer Center at the University of Arizona. He served as the 1992 campaign chairman for the Valley of the Sun United Way.

HOLIDAY WASSAIL

Simmer together for one hour:

2 qts. water

3 C. sugar

24 cloves

8 cinnamon sticks

8 allspice berries

After one hour (this makes the house smell real Christmasy), remove spices and add:

6 C. diluted frozen orange juice

4 C. lemon juice

4 C. apple cider

Wassail can be served hot or cold (best when hot). The apple cider can be cut with one half raw cider if available (for tangier flavor). It freezes well.

Mike Ritter

Mike Ritter

See "About the Artist" page 252.

CHOCOLATE EGG CREAM
(a la Brooklyn)

About 3 tsp. Fox' U-Bet® Chocolate Flavor Syrup

(You must use this brand! It's manufactured in Brooklyn, has the best flavor and is the key ingredient!

About 3 tsp. milk
About 8 oz. seltzer (unflavored, carbonated water)
1 - 12" salted pretzel rod

Pour syrup and milk into a 12 oz. glass. (A traditional shaped Coca-Cola® glass is preferred.) Stir the mixture with an iced-tea spoon.

Continue to stir while slowly adding the seltzer until the mixture reaches the top of the glass. You should have a nice "head" of foam which will provide you with a wonderful "moustache" as you drink.

Barbara Meyerson

Barbara Meyerson

Barbara Meyerson is the executive director of the Arizona Museum for Youth in Mesa. *"Everyone has heard of Brooklyn! It's a wonderful place filled with lots of people from lots of places with lots of rich traditions, lots of food and lots of wonderful tastes and smells. Growing up not far from the eastern shadow of the Brooklyn Bridge, some of my warmest childhood memories center around the soda fountains and the taste sensations they provided. First, you needed to dig into your pocket for some sweaty coins. Next you climbed atop a spinning stool and rested your elbows on an ice cold marble counter. Then, you ordered—a chocolate egg cream and a pretzel rod! Ah-h-h!"* You can see why Barbara is in the business of stimulating one's imagination—especially the little ones'! (Authors note: If you have never been through the Museum for Youth, do yourself a favor and go. It is a wonderful experience for all ages, and if you are looking for Barbara, she'll be the one with the friendly smile, enthusiastic laugh and perhaps even a foamy mustache!)

MOLLEN SHAKE

1 banana
1 C. fresh or frozen whole strawberries
1 C. plain nonfat yogurt
1 C. crushed ice
1 C. skim milk or more if desired
1 tsp. strawberry preserves

Combine all the ingredients in blender and blend until smooth. If shake is too thick, add small amount of skim milk until it is the consistency you desire.

Yields: about 1 quart
Serving size: about 10 ounces
Calories per serving: 132
Grams of protein per serving: 8
Grams of fat per serving: 0.5
Milligrams of sodium per serving: 106

Arthur J. Mollen

Art Mollen is the author of the 1978 bestseller, *Run For Your Life, The Mollen Method (1986)* and *Dr. Mollen's Anti-Aging Diet*, which made bestseller list in 1992. Dr. Mollen is the founder and medical director of the Southwest Health Institute in Phoenix, has lectured in the White House to the President's Council, and is a past member of the Governor's Council on Physical Fitness and Sports. Dr. Mollen has been a syndicated newspaper columnist for more than 12 years and has been featured on *"PM Magazine"* as well as in cover stories of "*Arizona Magazine*" and the "*D.O. Magazine*". He was resident doctor in 1984 on the ABC television show, *"A.M. Los Angeles"* with co-host Christine Ferrare. Appearances include *"The Larry King Show," "Good Morning America," "The Sally Jesse Raphael Show," "A.M. Canada Talk Show,"* and *"The Oprah Winfrey Show."* He has run more than 30 marathons, including 3 Boston marathons, and completed 10 triathlons.

GLÜG

1 gl. port wine
1 pt. grain alcohol
1 C. sugar

   Spices:
24 prunes
24 cloves
24 cardamom seeds, broken
2 C. raisins
6 cinnamon sticks
1 dried orange rind
10 almond nuts

Put spices in pan with enough water to cover fully. Cover and cook about 20 minutes. Heat wine in pan with lid. Add spices and water. Add sugar. Stir for a couple of minutes. Pour in alcohol. Keep heating the Glüg.

Light surface with match and let burn a minute or two. Extinguish by putting lid on pan. Reheat as needed. You may add wine, alcohol and sugar in the above proportions to spices as needed. Skol!!

Cliff Harris

Clifford Harris

Cliff Harris is a physician who works in management at CIGNA. He is Mesa's 1992 Man of the Year. Cliff is the founder of the East Valley Cultural Alliance and helped start the Mesa Senior Center. He serves on the boards of the Mesa United Way and the East Valley Community Foundation. He has helped to provide dental, eye, and wellness care for Salvation Army residents and homeless shelters. *"There are many mixtures for warm, sweet wine drinks, usually served at Christmas time, but Glüg has kept many a Viking from straying from home. It is particularly enjoyable on a cold evening. And a few people swear it cured their sinus trouble. Glüg is a traditional Scandinavian Christmas drink. One can savor the fragrance when entering the home with Glüg heating on the stove. It should be sipped in small quantities. Each Christmas a batch of Glüg is made and by adding the ingredients to the spices it can last through the Holiday Season! As with any alcohol drink, do not drive."*

Index

C - D

Desserts

L-M

Main Dishes

S - Z

ABOUT THE AUTHOR

Sandy Bruce is a Mesa homemaker, free lance writer and community volunteer. She is a native of Texas who moved to Arizona three years ago with her husband, Jeff Bruce, the executive editor of the Phoenix-area's Tribune Newspapers and her two children, Kacey and Logan. This is her first book.

The concept for *"What's Cookin' in Arizona"* originated when Sandy and a group of Arizona women visited Washington, D.C. in April 1992 to attend a luncheon honoring First Lady Barbara Bush.

Annie Rhodes, the wife of then-Congressman Jay Rhodes, R-Mesa, was the program chair. While there, Sandy acquired a copy of "The Congressional Club Cook Book," a hardbound, 600-page book packed with tantalizing recipes from members of Congress and their families.

"Why can't we do something like this for Arizona?" Sandy wondered. Thus was the idea for this book born.

In setting out to select the "cooks" for this volume, Sandy wanted to recognize both famous Arizonans, the folks who make the headlines, and also less well-known people who have made their own contributions to making the Grand Canyon State the best place to live in America.

When she isn't writing, Sandy devotes most of her time to her children and her community activities. She is a member of the Arizona Museum for Youth Guild, Mesa Leadership Training and Development Alumni, a board member of the Mesa YMCA, chairwoman of the East Valley Retired Seniors Volunteer Program Advisory Council, former member of the World Affairs Council of Arizona, is active in her children's PTO and is starting a Brownie troop soon!

ABOUT THE ARTIST

A native of Washington state, Mike Ritter moved to Arizona in 1983. He attended Arizona State University where he earned a Bachelor of Arts degree in History. More importantly, he spent the majority of his efforts in college working at the student paper, *The State Press*, where he drew editorial cartoons and a daily comic strip.

After ASU, Mike went to work for the Scottsdale Progress as editorial cartoonist. In 1992 he took the same position at the Tribune Newspapers for which Mike had drawn freelance cartoons during his college days.

Mikes loves history and politics and possesses an unshakable belief that he is always right. Mostly he loves cartooning. Actually its less of a love than an understanding that he has no other marketable skills.

See Mike's recipe for *Holiday Wassail* on page 252.

ARIZONA COOK BOOK

A taste of the Old Southwest! Sizzling Indian fry bread, prickly pear marmalade, sourdough biscuits, refried beans, beef jerky and cactus candy. By Al and Mildred Fischer. More than 250,000 copies in print!

5 1/2 x 8 1/2—144 Pages . . . $5.95

BEST BARBECUE RECIPES

A collection of more than 200 taste-tempting recipes. • Sauces • Rubs • Marinades • Mops • Ribs • Wild Game • Fish and Seafood • Pit barbecue and more! By Mildred Fischer.

5 1/2 x 8 1/2—144 pages . . . $5.95

CHILI-LOVERS' COOK BOOK

Chili cookoff prize-winning recipes and regional favorites! The best of chili cookery, from mild to fiery, with and without beans. Plus a variety of taste-tempting foods made with chile peppers. 150,000 copies in print! By Al and Mildred Fischer.

5 1/2 x 8 1/2—128 pages . . . $5.95

CITRUS LOVERS COOK BOOK

Tempting recipes for luscious pies, dazzling desserts, sunshine salads, novelty meat and seafood dishes! Plus tangy thirst-quenchers with oranges, grapefruit, lemons, limes, and tangerines. By Al and Mildred Fischer.

5 1/2 x 8 1/2 — 128 Pages . . . $6. 95

CHRISTMAS IN ARIZONA

'Tis the season . . . celebrate Christmas in sunny Arizona. Read about the fascinating southwestern traditions and foods. Create a southwestern holiday spirit with this wonderful cookbook. By Lynn Nusom.

6 x 9—128 pages . . . $8.95

SALSA LOVERS COOK BOOK

More than 180 taste-tempting recipes for salsas that will make every meal a special event! Salsas for salads, appetizers, main dishes, and desserts! By Susan K. Bollin.

5 1/2 x 8 1/2—128 pages . . . $5.95

CHIP & DIP LOVERS COOK BOOK

More than 150 recipes for making fun and festive dips. Make southwestern dips, dips with fruits and vegetables, meats, poultry and seafood. Salsa dips and dips for desserts. Includes recipes for making homemade chips. By Susan K. Bollin.

5 1/2 x 8 1/2—112 pages . . . $5.95

TAILGATE FEVER COOKBOOK

Your game plan to good eating . . . plus a helping of football savvy! Jam-packed with easy-to-prepare recipes and helpful football tips! The perfect gift for all football fanatics!

5 1/2 x 8 1/2—224 pages . . . $9.95

QUICK-n-EASY MEXICAN RECIPES

More than 175 favorite Mexican recipes you can prepare in less than thirty minutes. Features easy recipes for salads, soups, breads, desserts and drinks. Tips for quick preparation and recipes utilizing available ingredients. By Susan K. Bollin.

5 1/2 x 8 1/2—128 pages . . . $5.95

ARIZONA CROSSWORDS

If you love crosswords and Arizona, have we got a puzzle for you! 50 crosswords to challenge novice and expert alike. This is the way to learn about Arizona. Rivers, towns, native plants, historical figures, geography and much more!

8 1/2 x 11—64 pages . . . $4.95

ORDER BLANK

GOLDEN WEST PUBLISHERS

4113 N. Longview Ave. • Phoenix, AZ 85014

602-265-4392 • **1-800-658-5830** • FAX 602-279-6901

Qty	Title	Price	Amount
	Apple-Lovers' Cook Book	6.95	
	Arizona Cook Book	5.95	
	Arizona Crosswords	4.95	
	Arizona Small Game & Fish Recipes	5.95	
	Best Barbecue Recipes	5.95	
	Cactus Country	6.95	
	Chip and Dip Lovers Cook Book	5.95	
	Chili-Lovers' Cook Book	5.95	
	Christmas in Arizona Cook Book	8.95	
	Citrus Lovers Cook Book	6.95	
	Cowboy Cartoon Cook Book	5.95	
	Mexican Desserts & Drinks	6.95	
	Mexican Family Favorites Cook Book	5.95	
	Pecan-Lovers' Cook Book	6.95	
	Quick-n-Easy Mexican Recipes	5.95	
	Salsa Lovers Cook Book	5.95	
	Tailgate Fever Cookbook	9.95	
	Tequila Cookbook	7.95	
	What's Cookin' in Arizona	9.95	
Add $2.00 to total order for shipping & handling			$2.00

☐ My Check or Money Order Enclosed. . . . . $

☐ MasterCard ☐ VISA

Acct. No.   Exp. Date

Signature

Name   Telephone

Address

City/State/Zip

Call for FREE catalog

10/93   MasterCard and VISA Orders Accepted ($20 Minimum)

WhatsCkn

This order blank may be photo-copied.